Your
Horoscope
2020

....

Cancer

Your Horoscope 2020

....

Cancer

22nd June - 22nd July

barbra strisen - music

igloobooks

igloobooks

Published in 2019
by Igloo Books Ltd
Cottage Farm
Sywell
NN6 0BJ
www.igloobooks.com

0819 001.01
2 4 6 8 10 9 7 5 3 1
ISBN 978-1-78905-711-9

Written by Belinda Campbell and Jennifer Zelinger

Cover design by Dave Chapman
Edited by Bobby Newlyn-Jones

Printed and manufactured in China

CONTENTS
. . . .

INTRODUCTION
· · · · · · · · · · · · · · · ·

This horoscope has been specifically created to allow
you to get the most from astrological patterns and
the way they have a bearing on not only your zodiac
sign, but nuances within it. Using the diary section
of the book you can read about the influences and
possibilities of each and every day of the year. It will
be possible for you to see when you are likely to be
cheerful and happy or those times when your nature
is in retreat and you will be more circumspect. The
diary will help to give you a feel for the specific
'cycles' of astrology and the way they can subtly
change your day-to-day life.

THE CHARACTER OF THE CRAB

· · · · · · · · · · · · · · · · ·

Cancer is the cardinal sign that kicks off summer in the zodiac calendar, and is also the first of the Water signs. These summery Crabs love rounding up family and friends for a day at the beach. Creativity surrounds them, whether that means whipping up a meal for loved ones or redecorating the home. Cancerians saturate themselves with the latest trends in food, fashion, art and culture. They will have had that trendy new artist's work hanging on their walls long before anyone else can jump on the bandwagon. Or perhaps the masterpiece that Cancerians love most is their own, such as with artistic Crab Frida Kahlo. Their creative juices flow constantly and freely, and are born from a deep love and empathy.

For Cancerians, home is always where the heart is. Born in the fourth house signifying the home and family, they are best known for their unfailing love and caring nature. Some of the most beloved figures in history, such as Nelson Mandela and Diana, Princess of Wales, have been nurturing Cancerians. These homebody Crabs will usually make more of an effort than most to visit their family, wanting to surround themselves in loving and supportive atmospheres. Cancerians also love to invite people into their own home, hosting dinners, movie nights and plenty of parties – especially in their younger years. Friends and family should be careful of the crabby side, however. 'It's my party and I'll cry if I want' to

probably rings true for most Cancerians. They can be
overly sensitive, and are renowned for their almighty
moods. Security is what they crave, and the need to
settle their sometimes-unpredictable emotions.

THE CRAB

Tough on the outside yet vulnerable on the inside,
the Crab symbolises many of the key traits associated
with Cancerians. Those born under this sign have a
negative polarity, which can mean that they are prone
to processing thoughts and feelings internally, and
may retreat into the safety of their own shells for long
periods of time. Whilst their exterior may appear hard,
Cancerians reveal their soft sensitivity to those who
wait. A cosy and secure home life is an essential part to
their happiness. Whether they prefer to live alone like
the hermit crab or as part of a large family, Cancerians
often need to spend quality time on their own for some
peaceful self-reflection. With the love and support of
family and friends, they can be coaxed from whatever
sandy bay they may have decided to disappear into
temporarily. The Crab is a unique balance of strength
and vulnerability, which makes Cancerians treasured
family members and fiercely reliable friends or partners.

THE MOON

The mother of the sky and the guardian sign of the
zodiac calendar, the Moon and Cancerians share a
bond of emotional influence. The Moon is the closest
astronomical body to Earth, which is maybe why it feels
so familiar, and why it governs homebody Cancer. There

is a reassurance in being able to look up at the sky and watch the Moon's cyclical patterns, a constant quality that Cancerians are likely to find comfort in. The Moon's gravitational pull dictates Earth's tides, so any Water sign will feel the influence of the Moon greatly. For Cancerians, their emotional ties to home and family are where the maternal influence of the Moon comes into effect. Cancerians are best known for their caring side, but this can turn into a worrisome nature or a tendency to smother those closest to them if they become ruled by their emotions. Both male and female Cancerians have an emotional intuition that is unparalleled, thanks to the Moon's guidance.

ELEMENTS, MODES AND POLARITIES

Each sign is made up of a unique combination of three defining groups: elements, modes and polarities. Each of these defining parts can manifest in good and bad ways, and none should be seen to be a positive or a negative – including the polarities! Just like a jigsaw puzzle, piecing these groups together can help illuminate why each sign has certain characteristics and help us find a balance.

ELEMENTS

Fire: Dynamic and adventurous, signs with Fire in them can be extroverted. Others are naturally drawn to them because of the positive light they give off, as well as their high levels of energy and confidence.

Earth: Signs with the Earth element are steady and driven with their ambitions. They make for a solid friend, parent or partner due to their grounded influence and nurturing nature.

Air: The invisible element that influences each of the other elements significantly, Air signs will provide much-needed perspective to others with their fair thinking, verbal skills and key ideas.

Water: Warm in the shallows and freezing as ice. This mysterious element is essential to the growth of everything around it, through its emotional depth and empathy.

MODES

Cardinal: Pioneers of the calendar, cardinal signs jump-start each season and are the energetic go-getters.

Fixed: Marking the middle of the calendar, fixed signs firmly denote and value steadiness and reliability.

Mutable: As the seasons end, the mutable signs adapt and give themselves over gladly to the promise of change.

POLARITIES

Positive: Typically extroverted, positive signs take physical action and embrace outside stimulus in their life.

Negative: Usually introverted, negative signs value emotional development and experiencing life from the inside out.

CANCER IN BRIEF

The table below shows the key attributes of Cancerians. Use it for quick reference and to understand more about this fascinating sign.

SYMBOL	RULING PLANET	MODE	ELEMENT	HOUSE
The Crab	Moon	Cardinal	Water	Fourth

COLOUR	BODY PART	POLARITY	GENDER	POLAR SIGN
White/Silver	Breasts	Negative	Feminine	Capricorn

LOVE

....

Born in the fourth house of family and home, security can be essential to Cancerians in a relationship. Not ones for living a life made up of one-night stands, even though they might try it out in their younger years, they want to find a stable and long-term relationship. Family can be hugely important to Cancerians, so they will more often than not be asking whether they see themselves having children with potential partners on the first or second date. Whilst security is crucial, this isn't always the right approach for finding love. Leaving themselves open to vulnerability is an important practice for any hard-shelled Cancerians struggling to let love in.

Love is usually felt deeply and intensely by Cancerians. Being so in tune and receptive to both their own and their partner's emotions makes them some of the most intuitive lovers in the entire zodiac calendar. Cancerians often instinctively know what others need, without them having to express it. Such is their sensitivity, Cancerians will be mindful of always pleasing their lovers. This innate ability to pick up on what others want makes them hugely desirable.

Cancerians may be able to tap into emotions to form meaningful relationships, but this also has its disadvantages. They can be prone to emotional outbursts as damaging as a burst dam, or as irritating as a leaky tap. Whilst Cancerians that don't have a handle on their emotions should try to work on this, an empathetic spouse who won't take their partner's outbursts to heart will help bring balance. A steady Earth sign can complement Water perfectly, forming a nurturing and mutually beneficial bond. The cardinal aspect of Cancerians will usually make them happy to make the first move in love. They will also likely admire a fellow cardinal partner that matches their go-getter attitude.

ARIES: COMPATIBILITY 1/5

This pair shares opposite characteristics that don't always attract, sadly. A homely creature, the Cancerian may find the Arian's adventurous roaming too uncomfortable and unsettling. Conversely, the Arian will not thrive in this relationship if constricted or held back in any way by the Cancerian. However, these Water and Fire signs are true opposites, and therefore can stand to learn a great deal from one another. In particular, the Cancerian can teach the Arian to be more considered before acting, whilst the Arian can teach the Cancerian to be less worrisome.

TAURUS: COMPATIBILITY 5/5

Placed two positions apart on the zodiac calendar, a Cancerian and Taurean share a bond that can feel just like home. The Cancerian's frequent displays of love are deep and clear, like two names carved into a tree! The intensity of the Taurean's affection, mixed with the Cancerian's head-over-heels approach, can see these two lovers running to the altar and settling down with babies – not always in that order. Here are two signs that will do anything for each other, and will usually prefer their own little party of two.

GEMINI: COMPATIBILITY 2/5

This Air and Water pairing can feel too far apart personality-wise to make a good match, but the differences could actually prove to be strengthening. The Geminian is led by the mind and the Cancerian by emotion. These contrasting perspectives can lead to misunderstandings and arguments if the line of communication isn't clear. The Geminian can help the Cancerian communicate thoughts and feelings aloud rather than keeping them bottled up, while the Cancerian can provide lessons on the value of sensitivity. With so much to learn from one another, understanding and acceptance is vital to their success.

CANCER: COMPATIBILITY 4 /5

The love that two Cancerians have can run as deep and mysterious as the seas from which Water signs spring. The priority of creating a strong family home will be a shared goal for these two lovers, and building a large family unit will likely bring joy and satisfaction to them both. Co-parenting is something that this nurturing pair will likely excel at. With the right amount of personal space afforded to one another, these two will be able to keep their heads above water and enjoy exploring each other's depths.

LEO: COMPATIBILITY 3/5

Leo is ruled by the Sun and Cancer by the Moon,
so this pairing can feel as different as night and day.
However, the Lion and the Crab can also find that
they have plenty in common to form a lasting love.
Born in the fourth and fifth houses that partly signify
family and children, the Leonian and Cancerian share
a fundamental desire to find that long-term partner to
settle down with. Security is essential for the Cancerian
and the fixed side of the steadfast Leonian can provide
just that. This power couple could go the distance if
their differences are embraced.

VIRGO: COMPATIBILITY 3/5

A practical-minded Virgoan could be the balancing force
that a Cancerian needs in a partner. The Virgoan will
feel loved and protected by the nurturing Cancerian,
but by contrast the Cancerian can at times feel hurt by
the naturally critical Virgoan. Thanks to ruling planet
Mercury, the Virgoan's strong communication skills
should help them patch up any problems. The Earth
element in Virgo and the cardinal influence in Cancer
can make for a driven couple, so any loving ambitions
that these two share will likely be realised together.

LIBRA: COMPATIBILITY 3/5

Ruled by the planet of love and the emotions of the Moon,
the romance between a Libran and Cancerian can read
like an epic poem. The Libran's love for aesthetics will be
particularly attractive to the creative Crab, and encourage

many artistic endeavours. The home that these two could build together might well be a thing of beauty and harmony. Both cardinal characters, the Libran and Cancerian match each other's energetic attitudes, but may fight for power in the relationship. Whilst their introvert and extrovert tendencies could clash, the Libran's search for peace could help make this relationship last.

SCORPIO: COMPATIBILITY 2/5

These two Water signs could easily drown in a pool of emotion. Ruled by Mars, the Scorpian's passion for the Cancerian will be intense, and the Cancerian's feelings are highly likely to be mutual. Claws and stingers at the ready, explosive disagreements could see both sides getting hurt. Both can be stubborn and unwilling to bend in an argument, which may result in them parting ways quickly. However, once these two decide that they want to be together, they can experience a love that is unfailing in its loyalty.

SAGITTARIUS: COMPATIBILITY 1/5

A Cancerian might end up feeling lost with an adventuring wanderer that is a Sagittarian. The Sagittarian can help bring out a worldlier side to the Cancerian and show that a sense of community can stretch larger than the end of the road. With the Crab, the roaming Sagittarian can learn the benefits of settling down in a loving relationship. These two have contrasting Masculine and Feminine energies that can complement each other greatly, if their differences are

nurtured rather than discouraged. Plenty of personal
time needs to be allowed to reap the many rewards from
when opposites attract.

CAPRICORN: COMPATIBILITY 5/5

Opposites on the zodiac calendar, a Capricornian
and Cancerian can experience a tenacious love.
Symbolised often with a fish's tail, the Sea Goat that
represents the Capricornian can swim happily in the
Cancerian's warm waters. The Cancerian can indeed
help coax a playfulness from the Capricornian that
others don't always see. The Capricornian is ruled by
the authoritative planet of Saturn, so could be a strong
parenting partner for the family orientated Cancerian. If
these two hard workers fall in love with one another, the
dedication that they share could be staggering.

AQUARIUS: COMPATIBILITY 1/5

A rebellious Aquarian and security-seeking Cancerian
are not always an obvious match romantically. Whilst
their core character differences may be the cause of
arguments, if these two can find common interests that
can cement a foundation for friendship then love could
still bloom. If the Cancerian can help the intellectual
Aquarian to engage emotionally, then both could
mutually benefit from this unlikely but special meeting
of the heart and mind. Common ground to share and
foreign lands to explore will be what's needed for the
Aquarian and Cancerian to find a lasting love together.

PISCES: COMPATIBILITY 4/5

These two feminine and Water signs can be a vision of romance together. The Cancerian recognises the changeable river of emotion that runs within Pisces, and identifies with the alternating speeds, directions and temperatures. Here are two signs that enjoy nurturing loved ones, and so their love will be built on a mutual support system. However, the Crab and Fish need to be mindful not to get swept away by the floods of emotion they are both capable of unleashing in romantic relationships. If this is kept in check, then love and compassion can flow freely.

FAMILY AND FRIENDS

Cancerian homes are often as warm and as comforting as a cup of tea. Born into the fourth house that represents home and family, home life is of utmost importance to these expert nest makers. Cancerians will want to make their homes an inviting environment that all the family will feel comfortable and welcome in. Capricornians make for appreciative house guests, and will be sure to notice the new artwork hanging in the artistic hallway. Cancerians who have used their creativity to decorate their own home will find that it is not wasted on aesthetic-loving Taureans, who will be full of compliments. Both Cancerians and Taureans are very much homebodies, preferring to stay in and watch a film rather than party every night, so can make highly compatible housemates.

Earth and Water signs are considered to have a feminine energy and the deities associated most with the Moon are also female, so the relationships that Cancerians have with their mothers, sisters and female friends will likely help shape them greatly. Like most, the relationship with our parents plays a vital role in our overall happiness. For Cancerians, who are known for valuing family connections over most other things, this is especially applicable. Ask them to name a best friend, and they are most likely to name a parent. Cancerians likely want their own children at some stage and, if they are lucky enough to have them, will apply themselves wholeheartedly to parenting.

Cancerians are extremely intuitive beings, making them sensitive to the feelings of others. Friends and family of Cancerians might use them readily as a reliable shoulder to cry on. Cancerians are wonderful at giving loved ones reassurance and sensitive guidance, but they also expect these things in return. They can tend to dwell on the bad things that happen to them, and can hanker after constant reassurance when feeling low. When Cancerians feel like they are not receiving the sensitivity and comfort that they provide others, they can become defensive. Retreating inwards or reacting in an overly emotional manner are both typical of Cancerians that feel like they are being attacked. Their almighty moods and grudge-holding abilities can be exhausting and alienating. Peacekeeping Libran friends could help Cancerians to balance out their emotional outbursts, whilst friendly mutable Pisceans will be able to see past the mood swings. Friends, family and Cancerians themselves will do well not to dwell too readily on disagreements and practise forgiving and forgetting. The caring gestures that Cancerians are so good at showing should hopefully remedy arguments in the long run.

MONEY AND CAREERS

....

Being a particular star sign will not dictate certain types of career, but it can help identify potential areas for thriving in. Conversely, to succeed in the workplace, it is just as important to understand strengths and weaknesses to achieve career and financial goals.

For the Crab sign of the zodiac calendar, working in a social sector that helps to protect the vulnerable in society might be a natural calling. Whether it's working as police officers, firefighters or nurses, or other service roles, caring Cancerians thrive in a workplace where their protective instincts can be put to good use. Whether it is full-time work or a part-time passion, giving time to help others voluntarily can be an important part of their working life. Following in the footsteps of Cancerian philanthropist Diana, Princess of Wales, who was known for her kindness and charity, may be something that Cancerians wish to work towards.

Born in the fourth house that represents a love of home mixed with a Cardinal persistence, the writing profession is well suited to Cancerians. They possess the innate ability to understand emotion, and also translate it for others. Broody Cancerians should be careful of hiding away in their writing cave for too long though, as they are known for working themselves too hard. The cardinal aspect of Cancer gives this sign the driving force to leave a lasting and positive influence on the world. Seeing their words published could be a lifelong ambition for Cancerians and they may find great success, like fellow Crab Ernest Hemingway.

As with family, colleagues cannot be chosen. Therefore, it can be advantageous to use star signs to learn about their key characteristics and discover the best ways of working together. Creative and wonderfully empathetic, two Cancerians could find sharing their artistic talents an exciting collaboration. Whilst arguments could flare up, their ability to understand one another can get them back on track to working towards a shared goal.

Sea sponges for emotions, Cancerians soak up the positive and negative people in their lives, so working with the former can be essential. Optimistic Sagittarians could be just the positive colleagues to inspire less-secure Cancerians. A lack of confidence can hold this sign back professionally, so a 'fake it until you make it' attitude could do wonders for climbing the career ladder. Deep down, Cancerians are more than capable of rising to the top.

The organisational skills of the Crab are well known, and this attribute means that Cancerians are likely to succeed in their chosen career, regardless of whether they are working for someone else or managing their own business.

The satisfaction of a job well done is all this sign needs
to be motivated. Money itself is generally less of a
motivating factor – as long as their essential needs are
provided for, Cancerians are happy to sit back slightly
and spend more time with the people they love, rather
than clocking up the hours in the office chasing that
elusive promotion or bonus. This is certainly not to say
that Cancerians lack ambition or drive, simply that they
can be quite happy placing their focus on the home,
once their work is sorted.

HEALTH AND WELLBEING

Feeling things deeply, as Moon-ruled Cancerians do, means sometimes suffering from emotional insecurities and questions of self-doubt. If Cancerians find themselves sinking into anxiety, it may be that they are surrounded by too much negativity. They can be sponges for both positive and negative influences, so should review any problem areas and think how best to make improvements. A change of perspective may actually be what is required. For example, instead of wondering if they earn enough money, Cancerians should question how they can get a promotion at work. Trying to live life more fearlessly could help reduce some angst.

Spending time near water is the obvious way for Cancerians to unwind. Holidays by the coast, either home or abroad, help them to recharge their batteries and gain clarity on life. If running off to the sea isn't always feasible, taking a moment to go for a walk by a canal or pond can help them reflect on any concerns. Even a bubble bath can feel as restorative as a day at the spa.

Wellbeing practices need to be a particular priority for Cancerians. Wonderful at caring for others, they often neglect themselves. Physical exercise has been known to improve mental health and help reduce depression, and sports that lead Crabs to water, such as swimming or surfing, offer the dual benefits of both physical and emotional fitness. When exercise isn't possible, something as simple as watching a funny film could instead help lift their low moods.

Having a positive influence on the world should in turn have a positive influence on philanthropic Cancerians. Volunteering for a charity, or even setting one up, could be the legacy that they take the most joy in. They should be careful of shouldering the world's problems, however, to protect their own wellbeing. In order to truly help others, Cancerians should find and regularly practise ways of releasing worries before feeling overwhelmed. Having a place of peace and serenity in the home could help them let go of whatever stresses lay outside the front door. Weekly cleaning or decluttering sessions can also help Crabs feel more at ease.

Cancer

....

2020
DIARY PAGES

JANUARY

. . . .

Wednesday 1st
Happy New Year! You'll start 2020 with a sense of
adventure and exploration, which will mostly play out in
love. Explore, but stay aware and don't take it too far. It's
important that your gamble isn't on a fulfilling relationship.

Thursday 2nd
Mercury and Jupiter are conjunct in your house of
relationships and partnerships, and this area will be
highlighted over an extended period of time. The
result today is likely to be a major realisation hitting
you like a ton of bricks, and offering you a brand-new
perspective on love.

Friday 3rd
This is a very intense day for you. The Moon comes into
Aries, so issues may arise at work. Mars is on the end of
Scorpio making things feel edgy, and it will probably be
hard not to react when you are triggered. Try to observe,
and not give into, your feelings.

Saturday 4th

Relief is here, as Mars changes sign and moves into Sagittarius. It is time for you to take action regarding your health, habits and routines. Some changes are long overdue, so don't delay them any further. Take this opportunity and get straight to it.

Sunday 5th

This is a lovely Sunday for you, and you'll want to spend it in good company. Why not bake a cake and take it along to a friend's house? Once there, you'll have a lovely time enjoying a slice, sipping tea and soaking up all the news you receive.

Monday 6th

You start the week still in the mood for company, so make sure you enjoy lots of chats with colleagues and friends today. You crave intimacy too, so if there is a special someone in your life arrange a date or dedicated time together at home.

Tuesday 7th

During the next week, you'll have a strong sense that your relationships need to change. Whilst you are in a transitioning stage, and trying to determine the old from the new, go easy on yourself. This can be the start of an improved way to relate, but allow some time to mull it over first.

Wednesday 8th

The current conjunction of Saturn and Pluto is especially challenging for you, and it becomes about maintaining your individuality while being part of a couple. Relationships should be nurturing, as well as supportive. Do not give up on yourself. There are two sides to a coin, so aim at balancing both.

Thursday 9th

The energy is pretty high for others now, but you might feel the need to retreat and withdraw. You want only your trusted friends and family around, if anyone at all. Take time to be alone. There is no need to talk if you really do not want to.

Friday 10th

Today's Full Moon and lunar eclipse are very intense moments for you, as both take place in Cancer. It is especially important to Cancerians born between the 11th-13th of July. Today might be life changing, or be the catalyst for a transformative event. It all concerns self-knowledge and relationship insights.

Saturday 11th

Another shift of gears is taking place as the Moon
opposes the Saturn and Pluto conjunction. This is a
shift of structures, as well as your attempts to integrate
it emotionally. Uranus moves direct, so now all the
planetary energies are moving forwards. Old ground
is still being covered, but you finally feel as if you're
getting somewhere.

Sunday 12th

An incredible amount is going on, and this is a time
that can feel very intense. Please go easy on yourself.
The saving grace is you will start to understand what
this current restructuring is all about for you and your
relationships. There's no need to take action or make
judgements. Just observe carefully.

Monday 13th

The Sun joins the Saturn and Pluto conjunction,
bringing another layer to the shifts and changes you've
been experiencing recently. Venus, responsible for love
and relationships, intensifies this by being on the last
degree in your area of trust and intimacy. What new level
of affection are you reaching for?

Tuesday 14th

Take a breath today. Venus has moved into Pisces. For you, that highlights the magic flow of love, and inspires your fantasies and exploration mode. The Moon moves into practical Virgo, which for you has a lot to do with communication. From this evening onwards, you are ready to have some important conversations.

Wednesday 15th

You want to talk about your feelings today, and most likely with people nearest and dearest to you. Different topics might arise in these conversations, from the things that can be relied on, to the things that need to change. Just be open and avoid making criticisms.

Thursday 16th

A little surprise may come your way. It could be a friend who shares an inspiring travel idea or who supports you to otherwise explore. You are focussed on a home and family situation, whilst your mind is pondering relationships. It is a busy day and you could easily miss out an important detail.

Friday 17th

What is real intimacy? You'll be considering this question during the next three weeks. Allow all your thoughts to arise, even if they differ greatly from the so-called norm. Allow your unique viewpoint to form, without excluding other opinions.

Saturday 18th

The weekend starts busily, and there might be a key discussion with a friend. This could be about a secret that either you or your friend has kept, and it's time for it to be revealed. Try to find a creative solution that involves and serves everyone.

Sunday 19th

Leisure time, fun and play are highlighted today. If you have children in your life, this is the perfect opportunity to connect and engage with them. Dare to laugh loudly, and tune into the joy of just being. Enjoying yourself fully will recharge you, and it is well deserved.

Monday 20th

It's back to everyday business, which could literally mean work, chores or starting to invest in your health. You are ready to take definite action, but just make sure you don't overdo it. Avoid your tendency to focus too much.

Tuesday 21st

The Sun is now travelling through your area of shared resources, intimacy, taxes and transformation. This can be quite an interesting and intense time. Unusual events may occur, but that does not mean they are negative. Quite the opposite is true. Don't try to anticipate what might happen, and stay open for the experience instead.

Wednesday 22nd

Make sure you create the time and space for togetherness today. Don't let your responsibilities rule. You feel a need to connect, so being by yourself will not serve you – even at work. There could also be a tendency towards being needy. Take a step back if needed.

Thursday 23rd

Where do you want to grow in your relationships? That is today's theme. There is a need for feeling safe, but it is challenged by outer circumstances. Maybe you are unexpectedly asked to be present in a group setting. Just show up and try to make the best of it.

Friday 24th

Happy New Moon in Aquarius! You are planting the seed of a whole new level of intimacy and shared resources. For this seed to blossom, you must balance your inner masculine and feminine qualities. You need to learn to give and receive equally. Allow others to nurture you too.

Saturday 25th

Your mind is pondering the shared resources that feature within your day-to-day routine. You are ready and willing to take action in order to improve your situation. It is important that you dare to think out of the box and then act accordingly.

Sunday 26th

Your mind and feelings are in alignment, which makes for a well-balanced day. You might feel the urge to try something unusual, or even rebel against current structures and circumstances. You can handle this in either a constructive or destructive way. The choice is yours.

Monday 27th

Your intuition and fantasies are highlighted immensely during the next few days. If you can spend the day near water, maybe in a spa, this would be a perfect way for you to work with the energy. This will also help you to soothe and fulfil the need of being in an alternative reality.

Tuesday 28th

There is a strong urge to dive into daydreams and expand the reality beneath all boundaries.
If you can take another day off, or at least go slow and delay all tasks that need your structured focus, do so. You will be able to complete chores another day.

Wednesday 29th

Around midday, you will feel your sluggish energy
shifting and you'll suddenly be ready, willing and
determined to get everything done. This will play out
strongest at work. Focus your energy, and be amazed by
how easily you can get back on schedule.

Thursday 30th

Work is occupying the vast amount of your time. You
might find this especially challenging as your own
personal needs and those of your partner are hard to
meet throughout the day. Try not to worry about it too
much, and simply observe it. You will be able to find a
solution soon.

Friday 31st

January ends with some tension regarding outer
structures that are currently shifting. It is never easy
when you are in the midst of change, but it is worth
pushing through in order to move forwards and evolve.

FEBRUARY

· · · · · · · · · · · · · · · · · ·

Saturday 1st

As the Moon enters Taurus, you find yourself in a much
more grounded and stable mood. This feels great and
allows you to fully enjoy time with friends, or being
involved in a social event or meeting. Any plans you
make today are likely to change.

Sunday 2nd

You love to connect and be involved with people, but
how can you stay connected without losing yourself?
The answer is by developing healthy boundaries.
Implementing boundaries is today's challenge.
Protecting yourself first will ultimately allow you to
give to others.

Monday 3rd

You could feel like withdrawing inwards today, in
order to review the last few weeks. This is a time to
communicate through writing, and to note down
any out-of-the-box ideas. Just make sure you allow
yourself some me-time, no matter what your other
obligations might be.

Tuesday 4th

Mercury moves into Pisces, which means your thoughts turn to the future. This is supported by a nice aspect from Venus to Saturn, so you are actually preparing structures ready to make your vision tangible.

Wednesday 5th

You'll prefer to be alone today, but there is some action required regarding your everyday routine. It is the perfect time to improve your health regime. Try doing a workout DVD at home to combine the need to withdraw and the need for activity.

Thursday 6th

The Moon is now in your sign, so you will likely feel good and in your element. You may want to express yourself emotionally, and you really should. Also, remember that the Moon rules over ebb and flow. So just go with your own tide and embrace the feelings as they come and go.

Friday 7th

It is the final day of Venus in her exaltation of Pisces, so you could invest in your vision by beautifying and loading it with positive emotions. You also want to get a grip on your emotions in general, as the current shifts are a little hard to integrate. Focus more on nurturing yourself.

Saturday 8th

Venus has now moved into the tenth house, which is
your area of career, vocation and legacy. There is a major
focus in this area this year, but the greatest changes will
happen during the autumn and winter. The current task
is to observe your circumstances and ponder on what
would improve your situation.

Sunday 9th

Today's Full Moon highlights your values as well as your
possessions. Out of everything you own, what do you
hold dearest? Go through your cupboards and take a
look. If there are things that you do not love completely,
start to get rid of them.

Monday 10th

You begin the week with a desire to talk. Not for the
sake of just sharing any kind of information, but real
talk, where you share practical information that is useful
to you and your collocutor. It is okay to draw a line if
someone starts to gossip.

Tuesday 11th

You are still interested in real conversations, but you
want to have them with the people you live with. If you
need to reorganise your daily routine who takes the dog
out, does the grocery shopping or instate a regular date
night, these are all things to talk about now.

Wednesday 12th

Home is where the heart is. And, for you, home is where
safety is. So with the Moon entering your home space,
all you really want is to feel protected. This can be a little
tricky today, as there might be a situation where you are
asked to focus on your own needs first.

Thursday 13th

Your home is supposed to be safe and happy. What about
the current structures in your relationships? Are those
already aligned to support you in your home area, or are
there changes to be made? The real safety comes from
within, so make sure you do not compromise too much.

Friday 14th

Your mood changes from a more-balanced place to
an intense and probably very deep one. You need
this intensity to be able to express yourself creatively.
Embrace your feelings, whatever colour they are, but also
know that the people in your immediate environment do
not always feel with the same depth as you.

Saturday 15th

Mercury, who deals with the mind, logic and mental activity, is slowing down before going retrograde. Your mind is getting ready to deepen whatever you have been exploring so far. Do not take any action regarding your vision just yet, however, because there are more insights to come.

Sunday 16th

Mars, the planet of action, moves into your area of love and relationships. With this amount of planets and the nodes still there, this will be a very active time for you. The goal is to change your relationship patterns and dynamics for the better. This does not come easily, but the rewards will be incredible.

Monday 17th

Mercury is now moving backwards, and during the next three weeks you'll have the opportunity to re-evaluate your vision. Some of the ideas you have been pondering might seem impossible, too big or not big enough. Just be open to what will be revealed.

Tuesday 18th

A happy connection from Jupiter to Neptune expands your vision of relating to somebody. While Jupiter works as a magnifying glass, Neptune wants to dissolve boundaries. The result is that you are able to dream of the most loving and unconditional relationship.

Wednesday 19th

The Sun enters Pisces and supports your vision quest
and dreams. There is obviously something here yet to
be discovered that will have a tremendous impact on
your future. The best thing you can do is focus on your
intuition, and trust the messages you receive.

Thursday 20th

Relationships are highlighted, as the Moon is back in
that area. Here, it encounters Jupiter, Saturn and Pluto,
so it is likely to be a very active day with twists, turns
and contrary impulses. Make sure you stay in the present
moment and don't take things too personally.

Friday 21st

Mars has a very nice and flowing conversation with
Uranus today, so a surprise might come your way.
Perhaps a friendship will turn into something deeper or
more committed, or you'll see somebody in a brand-new
light. Whatever may happen, expect the unexpected.

Saturday 22nd

The weekend heralds a sudden turn of events too, as it is
now the Sun in flowing conversation with Uranus. This
could be about an opportunity to make your dreams
or vision happen with a friend, or even with a group of
friends or club you are involved in.

Sunday 23rd

The Pisces New Moon is here, and once again this is about your dreams for the future. It is a perfect day to make time for your new vision. You can start to build a vision board, collect pictures or write things down. However, remember that you will revise and expand your ideas throughout the year.

Monday 24th

Venus, the goddess of love, beauty and harmony, is facing a discussion with Jupiter. That means you might face a discussion with a colleague or business partner. It may actually be a good thing as your colleague or partner is favourable to you, and has good advice to give.

Tuesday 25th

This is not a usual Tuesday, but probably one you will remember in some way or another. Mars conjuncts the south node, which means you are asked to actively let go of old attachments and behaviours in your relationships. Do this for the sake of your own sovereignty.

Wednesday 26th

There is a lot of work to do today, and you want to get on with it. However, make sure you create some space to listen to your intuition. The Sun and Mercury are embracing, and during this you will most likely receive important information regarding your vision.

Thursday 27th

Today is quite busy, as some well-known tension arises between your work life and your relationships. This topic has come up before, so it is best if you do not allow it to throw you off. Keep focusing on the work you need to do.

Friday 28th

A wonderful and relaxing vibe arrives to give you a great start to the weekend. The energy is calm and solid, and you'll want to connect with your friends, invite them for dinner or go out and meet them in a restaurant. Don't stay at home and sit on the couch all on your own. Connecting to people is important.

Saturday 29th

It is an amazing day to connect, maybe by participating in a club meeting or by inviting friends over for dinner. An unexpected idea or insight might also be in the mix for you. However, if you make today all about work instead of leisure, this could really backfire and spoil your mood.

MARCH

....

Sunday 1st

The energy surrounding you is still chilled and relaxed.
It is perfect for a Sunday trip, maybe out in nature
encountering the first heralding of spring. It's also an
ideal day for recharging your batteries, and filling your
heart with joy and laughter. Enjoy.

Monday 2nd

You hopefully enjoyed the weekend just gone and all
the connections that were made. Today you are not
eager for company, so it is good if you can retreat – just
make sure others do not feel offended. They have done
nothing wrong, and neither have you. You just need
this time for yourself.

Tuesday 3rd

The Moon and Sun are having a discussion today, and
it is about bringing some logic to the plate. In order
for your dreams and visions to manifest, you must
not idealise to infinity. It is amazing to have a great
imagination, but flexibility and logic are needed in order
to build something worthwhile.

Wednesday 4th

You won't get bored today! The Moon enters your sign so you feel well. Elsewhere, Mercury returns to Aquarius, and you start to reinvestigate your shared resources and finances. The new ideas you have might be unusual, but try following them instead.

Thursday 5th

You have the opportunity to review your actions and reactions to the triggers your partner pulls. A conflict may arise, but how will you handle it? Do you want to take it personally, and get stuck in feeling offended, or will you try to find a solution right away?

Friday 6th

You are able to look at your emotional behaviour and attachments even more. Do you need the structure and safety from a lover or are you able to receive it from within? The task is not easy, but if you want to transform some of these patterns it is an amazing opportunity to do so.

Saturday 7th

As the Moon moves into your second house, you will most likely feel energised and joyful. If you can do something that involves fun and entertainment you can make it a perfect day. Why not go out to the theatre, a comedy show or a club?

Sunday 8th

This is a special Sunday, in which you can enjoy
an amazing connection to your intuition. Use this
opportunity to create space for reflection. If you'd rather
not do it alone, go to a retreat or event that focuses on
meditation or spirituality.

Monday 9th

Happy Full Moon in Virgo! This Full Moon highlights
communication, and the need to talk in an efficient
and direct way. You want to hear real facts and nothing
that is superficial or unnecessary. Choose your
conversations wisely, and this will be a good time to let
your fantasy meet reality.

Tuesday 10th

After yesterday's reality check, Mercury is pleased with
your progression and is ready to move forwards again.
Venus is making a nice angle to the north and the south
node, so you will likely feel supported by friends if
you're planning on trying something for the first time.

Wednesday 11th

Your home and family life comes into focus and,
with Saturn on the final degree in your house of
relationships, there is a deep urge to find time for
your loved ones. Do the recent circumstances allow
for enough interaction or are they restricting you?
Take a close look to see if current structures still
serve everyone.

Thursday 12th

Around midday, the Moon changes sign and your emotions may intensify. Make sure that you create an outlet for them. If you feel full of joy, make sure you express it and have fun. If you feel sad or angry, talk to a friend, dance, write or paint. Don't suppress your feelings.

Friday 13th

It is likely that you'll feel a lot throughout the day, perhaps more so than usual. You will find great support and grounding through connecting with family, co-workers or your key social groups. This should be a happy and flowing day for you, so make the most of it.

Saturday 14th

The weekend is here, and it starts with a great day to work on your vision board. You are set up to express creatively, you are willing to act upon your dreams and you are able to notice what must change in order for your vision to bloom.

Sunday 15th

Take a look at your health today. Maybe your food choices have not been the best recently. If you have not been taking the time to cook vegetables, and have instead just been putting junk food in the microwave, you may want a change. Cooking is also a great way to spend more time with your partner.

Monday 16th

Mercury is back in Pisces, allowing your mind to once again focus on the dreams, visions and ideas you wish to explore. This is the final time, and what you think about now is most likely to form your actions in the near future. You will, however, cover old ground first.

Tuesday 17th

Uranus, the planet of awakening, rebellion and surprises, is in a harmonious contact to both the south and the north node. Get ready for some unexpected shifts and changes. Do not worry, they will all be in your favour – right away and for the foreseeable future.

Wednesday 18th

It is a busy day in regards to your love life, and authority figures. Stay as calm as you can, and find your inner strength and security. Support yourself by staying grounded in the morning and throughout the day. Deep breathing can be a simple and effective method for doing so, wherever you are.

Thursday 19th

As the Moon moves into Aquarius, you'll crave a change. Maybe you can do something exciting today? This could be as simple as reorganising your schedule. Take an alternative route to work, maybe go by train instead of driving, or spend your lunch break outside. Allow this day to be different.

Friday 20th

Happy spring equinox! The Sun moves into Aries which not only marks the beginning of spring, but for you also means focusing on your work, reputation and legacy. Mars and Jupiter are embracing today, starting a brand-new cycle for expanding your relationships. Exciting times are ahead.

Saturday 21st

The Moon is currently travelling behind the Sun, so your emotional energy comes back to focusing on your vision. You are now aligned emotionally and mentally about all that you wish to pursue in life. This interesting time also heralds the possibility to connect work and your vision. Don't be afraid to take a small step into the unknown if it means following your heart.

Sunday 22nd

Today, your mind aligns with the north node. This helps you to find an improved sense of self within your vision, one that you couldn't see before. Saturn has left your area of love, allowing you to look back at 2019 and the ways your relationships have changed. However, the story is not over yet. What comes next in life's journey for Cancer?

Monday 23rd

This week starts off with two very different dynamics, as Mars comes together with Pluto. This means you could be challenged through a trust issue or a very personal conflict. Some disillusion might be involved. Try to keep a clear head and trust your ever-powerful intuition.

Tuesday 24th

The Aries New Moon is here, and it could mark a time of new beginnings in your career or a new focus on your legacy and reputation. You will be able to start afresh and with a renewed vigour, be it at work or any of the social clubs to which you belong.

Wednesday 25th

What changes in your career or public life could support your development? Is it getting back into work life, or could it mean working less? Whatever it is, make sure it gives you a greater sense of self. Security should come from within, and give you the confidence to make your own decisions.

Thursday 26th

It is the time of the month where you love to connect the most, at least regarding bigger groups. Today, there could be unexpected delays or changes to your plans. It is not a relaxed day, but rather one where you might have to bite your tongue. Focus on love.

Friday 27th

You should take the opportunity to connect and enjoy time with your friends today. What about a dinner party at home or going out to an expensive restaurant? You typically favour a stylish setting and the best food. You would never abandon a sense of luxury, would you?

Saturday 28th

Venus is in a loving conversation with Jupiter today, which might help you to meet new people or deepen existing friendships. Either way, you will feel safe and secure relating to these people, and they will honour and value the relationship as much as you will.

Sunday 29th

This is a Sunday made for me-time. What could you do to recharge and focus solely on yourself? If you have children, ask a friend or relative to take care of them today. Use the free time to do something fun or relaxing. Some space will do you good.

Monday 3oth

Today could feel busy and edgy, because Mars is sitting on the final degree of Capricorn. For you, that could mean that there are some issues coming up within one-to-one relationships. The issues could be personal, or they could be about a job. The tension will dissolve quickly, so just breathe.

Tuesday 31st

Mars enters Aquarius and encounters Saturn on the doorstep, presenting you with questions around shared resources, finances or intimacy. Anything unusual suddenly seems incredibly appealing. You like to challenge the status quo and find brand-new solutions to problems, so you are well equipped to overcome any current restrictions.

APRIL
....

Wednesday 1st
The Moon is in your sign and in a very positive connection to Neptune and Mercury. Your thoughts and feelings are in harmony, and you think about a higher vision of yourself. This new you may be challenged by your public or work life. How can you serve and act in the outside world while remaining true and authentic to your core?

Thursday 2nd
As the Moon moves into Leo you focus on both your self-worth and self-expression. With the Sun currently focused in your sector concerning career and legacy, it is likely that you will now be presented with an exciting opportunity to translate an idea into a reality. Go and have fun.

Friday 3rd
Venus, the planet of love, beauty and harmony, has been beautifying connections with your friend and social circles. Now, as she ingresses Gemini you start to focus more inwardly. Take care of yourself every day, and do yourself good. If you can arrange a spa visit or a retreat, that would be perfect as well.

Saturday 4th

How do you relate to yourself, and how do you relate to others? What are you hiding deep inside that you could share with someone you trust? What would you never ever share? Your mind is exploring dreams and fantasies, so it is likely that you cannot see clearly right now.

Sunday 5th

While your mind is in a fantasy land, your emotions are focused on reality. Jupiter and Pluto meet for their first embrace. They want to help you expand and transform your love life for the better. They will meet again, so whatever comes up next will probably evolve further.

Monday 6th

You are able to connect emotionally to where your relationship expansion could serve you. You are able to intuit and feel what will work and what won't. It is likely that you can go and practise something new immediately. Even if this is not the final result, experience beats vision.

Tuesday 7th

You already have an intuitive understanding of the upcoming shift, and today you can also add a mental note to that. From the safe space of home, you are able to act fearlessly and are open to brand-new insights. An issue of trust with friends could arise unexpectedly.

Wednesday 8th

Happy Full Moon in Libra! This Full Moon highlights
your home and family environment. Your home is
your safe and protected space, where you retreat and
recharge. Is there something else needed to make it even
more your castle? Take care of it right away to improve
your flat or house.

Thursday 9th

Intensity is high today. This is true emotionally, and in
regards to outside influences. You may find it hard to
take the right actions and to find a balance between your
own need to express and the demands and restrictions
you face in your social circle. A brand-new approach
offers the highest resolution potential.

Friday 10th

Venus will soon move retrograde, giving you plenty of
time to work on your innermost self. This is a perfect
opportunity to start a journal, and to see which internal
voices ask for your attention. The personal work you
do now will come up again in the future, but to offer a
different perception.

Saturday 11th

Mercury moves into your area of work, business and legacy, and you try to make sense of how to best integrate that in your daily routine. If you have been procrastinating, take the opportunity to do the small jobs first. While you do so, think about how you could optimise your productivity for the maximum effect.

Sunday 12th

You might have a great idea about how you could use some shared resources for the improvement of your own career or legacy. Before you tell others, make sure it is a win-win situation and everybody gets something out of it. If you are able to get everyone onside, you can lay a great foundation.

Monday 13th

The Moon once again highlights all your relationships, so make sure you have some spare time to spend with your partner or close friends. Make sure both of your needs are met and do not compromise too far. This is the greatest challenge of all, but you keep getting better at it.

Tuesday 14th

A change is needed in order to align your relationships with your job, and you feel that very intensely today. You might not yet know how everything must transform, so just observe and take some notes. Also, ask your partner about his or her wishes.

Wednesday 15th

The Sun and Jupiter are in a tense conversation today, but you will be able to work it out. Maybe there are new colleagues at work, or you need to contact new customers. Do not be afraid of the expansion, you will get to everyone over time and all will work out fine.

Thursday 16th

You can connect to a trustworthy person today and reveal your innermost self to them. The perspective the other person offers differs from your own and will broaden your horizons. You have the opportunity to see yourself in a new light, and that will support your investigations further.

Friday 17th

When was the last time you took a look at your vision? It is important to look at it regularly in order to manifest it, and when the Moon enters Pisces is the perfect monthly opportunity for you. Dream as if your vision could be true. How would you feel if it were real? Savour this vibe.

Saturday 18th

Today you think about what you could achieve, and try to align this with insights about yourself. Perhaps much more is possible than you believed until now. Let your mind run wild. What would you like to achieve or initiate? Where could you complete pioneering work?

Sunday 19th

As soon as you figure out what you want to achieve today you will be able to take some action. This will likely involve at least one other person that is willing and able to support you along the way. Isn't it amazing that you don't have to do it all alone?

Monday 20th

The Sun has now moved into your area of friends and social circles. You will likely be more involved in these groups, or even find new ones during that transit. Your energy levels might be low today, as the Moon is coming into its balsamic phase. Take a rest if you need to.

Tuesday 21st

What resources can you rely on in order to work and connect in your social groups and circles? You will really ponder this question today, and create new ideas about why it is important, useful and necessary to join forces. A certain power lies in unity that allows everyone to be stronger.

Wednesday 22nd

Today's energy is low, which is somewhat hard to handle. You want to take action, move forwards and even push things, but you're restricted with this limited amount of energy. Go easy on yourself. You can only do as much as is possible, and that is surely enough.

Thursday 23rd

Here is the Taurus New Moon. It signifies new beginnings in regards to friends, groups and social environments. You may meet new people, join new groups or connect on a new level. This is true both on and offline. Whoever you want to connect to, make your first steps.

Friday 24th

No matter if you check in with new or existing groups today, the most important thing is to go and connect. Enjoy the company, safe space and a good time. With the sign of Taurus involved, there is also a chance for some really good food.

Saturday 25th

You want to withdraw today and think about some very important changes that you now know to be imperative. These changes include either your priorities or the power your relationships have upon your career and legacy. You are thinking about ways to be more self-sufficient.

Sunday 26th

Pluto, the planet of change and transformation, starts its retrograde cycle. Just as you were thinking about self-sufficiency, you will discover what needs to change during that retrograde. The Sun joins Uranus today, and this can manifest as a sudden opportunity brought to you by one of your friends.

Monday 27th

Today you want to retreat and be alone. Take this time off, as you need it to recharge. During the next few weeks, you will want to be in continual contact with people. Your mind is focusing on this area in your life, now that Mercury moves into Taurus.

Tuesday 28th

This is the last time that the Moon crosses the north node in your sign. The story comes to a close. What is the last improvement that you want to make? Now that you know the greatest security lies within, and not without, you can act freely and with more self-confidence.

Wednesday 29th

Balance is the key. You want to achieve harmony between your needs and the demands of others. It is a long road towards perfection, even though you have already learnt a lot. Give value to your own feelings and know that it is okay to nurture, and also to be nurtured back.

Thursday 30th

You could be a little selfish today, even though you know that sharing is caring. You may be eager to keep your emotional needs, and resources, to yourself. If you do share, make sure the lucky recipients honour the value of all that you offer. Do not be used.

MAY

. . . .

Friday 1st

You will draw an amazing conclusion about your friends and social circles today. It is like a light bulb shining suddenly so brightly that you cannot miss it. You know whom you want to connect to and you are willing to make the necessary moves right away.

Saturday 2nd

How about a short trip this weekend? It would be great to see something different and spend some time in nature, now that everything is starting to flower and blossom. It could be a wonderful and joyful time of communication and laughter, and you would be able to be a good listener too.

Sunday 3rd

All of life's energies are flowing smoothly, and you can connect harmoniously with your partner, family or friends. However you choose to spend time with others, make sure you enjoy this grounded, earthy vibe, as well as the beauty of nature. It will be the perfect retreat.

Monday 4th

The Moon moves into your area of home, and you enjoy
being back in your own surroundings. Mercury joins
the Sun for another hug, and it is like receiving a new
instruction. This is again about the groups and friends you
are becoming involved with. What if one of the groups
proves to be of even more value than you already thought?

Tuesday 5th

This is a major day. The nodes end the cycle they
began in Cancer and Capricorn back in November
2018, and shift into Gemini and Sagittarius. A major
transformation in the way you nurture yourself, and
how you become more self-sufficient and independent
should be expected.

Wednesday 6th

The Moon in Scorpio is always about intensity and,
for you, it is best if you are able to express it. This can
be through art, dance, music or anything creative. No
matter what colour your feelings are, dare to show them.
This can even inspire others to connect more to their
own feelings. You can be a role model here.

Thursday 7th

Today's Full Moon brings the year's highest and
brightest amount of Scorpio energy, so do not allow the
limitations of others to hold you back. You may want
to play, have fun, express yourself or enjoy a romantic
evening. Whatever you do, go all in and embrace it fully.

Friday 8th

Now that the south node has moved into Sagittarius,
you have the opportunity and the need to make some
changes in your health or nutrition. You may also
consider getting a new pet. Your routines and daily
habits are about to change, so start to think about what
is no longer serving you.

Saturday 9th

There is still a great flow of energy, and today it flows
harmoniously between Mercury and Pluto. The theme of
power and transformation in your social groups arises.
You can use your power in a way to support everyone,
and including your beloved might also help bring a
necessary change to the group.

Sunday 10th

Your love life is highlighted, and you will start to think about expanding your relationships. Once again, there could be new people showing up in your life or existing bonds could deepen. Just make sure to have some boundaries in place while you remain open for a deepening. One thing does not rule out the other.

Monday 11th

Saturn dared to test the Aquarian air first. He now ends his trip to lay the final foundations and structures to get you ready for your next story. The focus on your relationships will intensify for the last time, leaving you then ready to work on the new.

Tuesday 12th

Mercury comes home into Gemini, and the Moon moves into Aquarius today. Lots of air energy means lots of mental activity. During the next few weeks, you will be able to think quickly but might have trouble focusing. For you, it is more about pondering your innermost self and secrets than about outer events and experiences.

Wednesday 13th

This week is really busy. Today Venus starts to move retrograde, which means she gets ready to end one cycle and begin the next. You dive deep into your subconscious to start a journey of exploration. Mercury, also in Gemini, is helping you to find reasonable logic in this process.

Thursday 14th

Mars in Pisces is about dreams and visions. You will best discover yours by searching within, before trying to realise each one. Your only task, for now, is to create a space that allows you to think. Isn't it great to be granted permission to dream?

Friday 15th

There is yet another shift today. Now Jupiter, the planet of expansion, decides to move backwards in order to look at everything he recently magnified and expanded. This brings the chance to review, and possibly make new choices, about any developments you may be unhappy with.

Saturday 16th

The way you feel about your fantasies and visions could come into conflict with virtues you never knew you had until now. It can be unsettling to discover new features about the self. Stay compassionate, and be loving and forgiving with yourself. What is brought to light can soon start to grow.

Sunday 17th

The first half of Sunday has a dreamy vibe, but the second half asks for action. You suddenly feel a surge of energy, and can get many things done. Use the energy to your advantage, even if it means doing things you usually would not do on a Sunday.

Monday 18th

You feel brave and courageous, so dare to dive into your subconscious to encounter those parts of yourself that are usually hidden. Your clear, logical perception makes this so much easier for you. If you can stay compassionate and forgiving about what you discover, you will be able to receive some great treasures.

Tuesday 19th

Your emotions align to Venus retrograde and everything that she is digging up. This is more about your female and yin side. You want to see the polarities inside yourself. We do not only hide shadows from ourselves, but also our light. What light do you hide that wants and needs to be seen?

Wednesday 20th

It is amazing how astrology works. As the Sun moves into Gemini, you'll receive even more support while working on your self-discovery. Elsewhere, the Moon sits in Taurus, which helps you connect with friends. These meetings will also aid your mission to understand the self.

Thursday 21st

Usually when the Moon is in Taurus, you love nothing more than meeting up with family and friends. If that's not the case this month, do not be alarmed. You are doing lots of inner work and the New Moon is coming up, which often makes you feel deflated and tired.

Friday 22nd

Here comes the New Moon in Gemini, in the midst of a Venus retrograde. Usually, the New Moon is a time to set an intention and to plant a seed. For this cycle, however, the suggestion is to expect the intention to shift and change until the Venus retrograde is complete.

Saturday 23rd

Mars is still in Pisces and dives into your dreams and visions. There is a tense aspect of your self-discovery. What if the vision you created is in conflict with parts of yourself? The answer is easy, you need to be honest and possibly adjust the vision.

Sunday 24th

It is the first time that the Moon crosses the new north node in Gemini. This is a hint that your subconscious will be a topic for a long period of time. Eighteen months to be precise. Helpfully, a lot of the work starts right away.

Monday 25th

With the Moon in your sign, it is a day to feel good and enjoy the flow of energy. If you can spend time swimming or maybe walking by a river or the sea it will top your mood, and you will literally be in your element.

Tuesday 26th

An issue might come up with a loved one today, and it is likely to be about trust and intimacy. If you can observe the situation, and not let your feelings overwhelm you, you will be able to solve the situation quickly and without unnecessary drama. It is probably not nearly as bad as it seems.

Wednesday 27th

The Moon in Leo can stand for dramatic emotions, but also for fun and entertainment. How you wish to manifest that energy is up to you. Better to find a constructive and happy way than to get involved in drama, don't you think? Show off all of your positivity today.

Thursday 28th

Mercury has been rushing through Gemini and is now entering Cancer, where he will stay for a long time. This gives you the chance to get to know yourself better. However, it is not about your subconscious, but about your whole persona and how you want to be perceived in the world.

Friday 29th

Time for a reality check. This is the time of the month when you can be pragmatic and productive, and are far less likely to become overwhelmed by your emotions. You are probably very grounded now. Use this energy to get things done and to make decisions.

Saturday 30th

Do you remember the intention you set at the New Moon? Now is a time to be realistic about it and make adjustments. There is still much more to be revealed to you, but your actions should already be grounded in reality and not in a fantasy land.

Sunday 31st

You end the month focused on your home and family life. It is a great day to enjoy the privacy of your own four walls, and to recharge after what has been a busy and intense month. Cuddle up in your safe space and indulge in your family. Just relax.

JUNE
·················

Monday 1st
You feel at home in yourself, and that is well supported
by being in your actual home space and being
surrounded by your family. With everything that's
currently going on, it is necessary to sometimes retreat
so that you have a chance to integrate all the changes.

Tuesday 2nd
Venus retrograde enters Mars. You feel as though
there is a huge tension between your innermost
self and what you thought about yourself before. It
is like disillusionment, which is not a comfortable
experience. Yet it can be very liberating to be honest
and truthful with yourself.

Wednesday 3rd
Your sense of self-expression is fully aligned with your
mind, so you know exactly what you want to say. With
Uranus in opposition, this expression could be sudden
and spontaneous. Be sure not to suppress anything.
Venus meets with the Sun, so there could be major
insights into your new and emerging self.

Thursday 4th

There is a tension between your everyday routines, the new emerging insights about yourself and the vision you want to follow. In order to align each part, it is important that you ground yourself in reality first. Once your basic needs are met you can expand out further again.

Friday 5th

Happy Full Moon in Sagittarius! This Full Moon illuminates what is necessary for you in regards to health, nutrition or daily work. You are invited to explore these areas with a new curiosity, as well as the willingness to let go of old beliefs and behaviours.

Saturday 6th

What feelings emerge when you think about your dreams and visions? Are you afraid to dream too big or too much? Big dreams can help you move forwards in life, but try to feel your way to that dream. Let your intuition guide you, instead of your mind.

Sunday 7th

When was the last time you created the space for intimacy? You are in a phase where you are doing much inner work, and your partner's needs may have been forgotten. It is a great day to say thank you for all the support and presence. Nurture your relationship.

Monday 8th

You could be surprised by the depth of a relationship and feel immensely grateful that there is still much more possible. Be sure to let your beloved know just how much you appreciate them. If you don't want to say it aloud, write a heartfelt letter or note.

Tuesday 9th

You may want to enjoy some hours of real intimacy today. This could be through physical affection or very honest and open talks. Intimacy in itself is multilayered and requires trust in the first place. What do you want to trust someone with? Are you open for someone to trust in you?

Wednesday 10th

The Sun square Neptune can be a day when you are suddenly waking up from a beautiful and colourful fantasy. It could also be about something that remains hidden for now or something that you idealise. Either way, the truth is about to be revealed, and that is always for the highest good.

Thursday 11th

Your intuition runs high as you journey further into dreams and visions. You feel there is something profoundly beautiful within them. It might seem other-worldly, but yet you suspect there is something about it that could be true. Don't stop dreaming.

Friday 12th

Today you have the opportunity to connect to your inner core. When you get up in the morning, try to remember your dreams and note down whatever comes to mind. Sometimes, a dream can hold an important message. Use your intuition for interpretation, instead of looking the meaning up in a book or online.

Saturday 13th

The topic of dreams and visions remains very important. Today is particularly significant, as you could make the first real step of manifesting your dream into reality. Just follow the signs and synchronicity, and your next step will appear magically in front of you.

Sunday 14th

This week has been so different from usual, you really want to end it with something that makes you feel alive. Let this be a day full of activity and action in the world. You may even have an event to attend that puts you centre stage in public.

Monday 15th

You feel impatient and want to accomplish a lot. With everything you do today, ask yourself how the world perceives you and if you do care about that. Your mind will ponder this thought for some days, which is a little unusual, but over time you will receive clarity.

Tuesday 16th

In the first half of the day, you may feel introverted and self-centred. Make sure you go out to meet friends in the afternoon or evening to bring balance to the situation. The conversations you have may also help you to receive further insights. Sometimes we need others to mirror us in order to see ourselves clearly.

Wednesday 17th

Today you want to connect to as many people as possible, so it is the perfect opportunity to hold a team meeting. You are able to listen to everybody and could be the uniting force if there are any differences of opinion. Don't be afraid to speak up. You will see that your dedication is highly appreciated.

Thursday 18th

Mercury starts its retrograde motion. This gives you an ideal opportunity to think about yourself and your persona in greater depth than you usually would. It is not selfish to do so. In fact, it is ultimately selfless. After all, the better you can nurture yourself, the better you can nurture others, too.

Friday 19th

This is not just any Friday. The Sun is crossing the north node, which may illuminate something deep inside of you never seen before. Stay in observation mode until it presents itself. Once the insight is revealed, your future pathway will become clearer – much to your delight.

Saturday 20th

You have been thinking about your dreams and visions for a while now, and are ready to act upon them in regards to expanding your relationship. You might be very happy today as you start to feel how it all might come together. Invite your partner for a wonderful summer night out.

Sunday 21st

The summer solstice and the New Moon solar eclipse happen back to back today. It is a powerful moment for you in particular, so just close your eyes and make a wish. Make a request about your future self and the love you want to bring to the world. It is time to share your gift.

Monday 22nd

It is like you are on cloud nine today. You feel the beauty of the world, and fully embrace the summer air, sunbeams, flowers and butterflies. If it's possible, take the day off or make it a shorter working day. Wherever you are, be sure to spread your good mood.

Tuesday 23rd

Neptune, the planet of dreams, fantasies and illusions, starts his retrograde motion today, so your dream life could be even more vibrant and lively. Sometimes we receive messages through our dreams. Start a dream journal and write down everything you remember as soon as you wake up.

Wednesday 24th

It is a great day to treat yourself. Why not invest in a statement outfit? You don't need to hide away. Show everyone what you buy and, in turn, who you are. You could also pick something for your house or home. The most important thing is to buy what you love.

Thursday 25th

Venus moves direct today. It has been an intense ride, with you discovering so much of yourself that was hidden and buried. During the next five weeks, you have time to integrate everything you've discovered. New, and necessary, ways of communicating will also open up.

Friday 26th

Mars crosses a special point in the zodiac. A memory of an old hurt or emotional wound may come up, but the great thing is you realise that you have healed. You now hold some kind of medicine to help others, and you might get a chance to do exactly this today.

Saturday 27th

Today you want to bring unconditional love to the world. You could sponsor a friend taking part in a fun run, donate old clothes or help in a soup kitchen. It is important to you to do something that makes a real difference. Find the cause you want to support today and act.

Sunday 28th

Tension could arise in your home or with your family today. For the remainder of the year, you will focus much of your energy on the outside world and your family may sit in opposition. Do not worry, you will eventually reconcile and find a way to suit everyone.

Monday 29th

You might find yourself in an argument with your partner. While you discuss the future of your home life, make sure both of you listen carefully to each other's needs and wants. If you focus on finding a solution, and not on who is wrong or right, it will turn out fine.

Tuesday 30th

Today is the second meeting of Pluto and Jupiter. This means you are willing to make further changes in your relationship, as long as they help each of you to grow and evolve. Magical and beautiful things can happen if you open up, and it could transform more beautifully than you imagined.

JULY

....

Wednesday 1st
Your inner core is aligned with your mind today, so you
are able to view yourself from a very unique perspective.
Others will see you quite differently. Trust your partner
by sharing these insights and your experience. This will
deepen and strengthen your bond.

Thursday 2nd
Saturn returns to Capricorn, and with this you are
willing to release old, limiting structures. You create
space for new ones that will serve you in a deeper and
closer way. You might want to make sure that you take
care of daily business today as well.

Friday 3rd
Today is quiet in its nature, which is very welcome after
all the intense energy you've been dealing with lately. If
the intensity has prevented you from attending to daily
demands, today is the perfect day to catch up. You might
actually find otherwise mundane tasks soothing.

Saturday 4th

This weekend, you only want to focus on love and relationships. This would be a great opportunity for a short trip, home or away, to enjoy summer to the fullest. Whatever location you choose, enjoy the intimacy and the feeling of belonging. Take a photograph to capture this special time.

Sunday 5th

Today's Full Moon in Capricorn highlights your relationships, and you can spend a wonderful and magical night under the moonbeams. If you want to be more committed in your relationship, this would be a great day for a marriage proposal. Alternatively, discuss renewing vows if you're already married.

Monday 6th

You are high on love and start the week in this wonderful vibration. If you are on holiday, you will likely have an especially good time. If you need to work, you'll have the most impact on projects that bring people together. Help to connect and create win-win situations.

Tuesday 7th

You are not as connected to your feelings and intuition as you usually are, so are therefore approaching things more from a logical and unique perspective. This might feel somewhat strange for you, but sometimes it is good to detach a little to gain more clarity.

Wednesday 8th

You want to move forwards with your career, but before you act you should be clear about what self-actualisation means to you. There might be a new position available and everything looks quite safe. However, what is it that you truly desire? Will it support you in your growth?

Thursday 9th

You ponder about so many important things, the universe hardly allows for a break. Today, you could enjoy some respite if you choose to see a movie, read a novel, visit a museum or go to an art gallery. Anything that supports your imagination is a welcome, and deserved, break.

Friday 10th

Your imagination is running high. Have another look at your vision board. Since the year started you have been working on it a lot, so what is the current status? If you want to get creative with it or add other destinations and details, now is the time.

Saturday 11th

Although it is the weekend, you do not want to rest. Instead, you long to be out and active. Should you need to work, it will be easy for you and you will most likely enjoy it. Either way, you should keep yourself busy and focused more on the outside world.

Sunday 12th

This is a beautiful day that supports your dreams and nurtures your vision. You received the last bit of clarity regarding your self-actualisation recently, and can now align this perfectly with a higher cause and calling. Spending time at the sea or near a pool would be perfect too.

Monday 13th

You seek connections this week, so make sure you have plenty of coffee or dinner dates with your friends planned in. It is likely that they can help you in regards to your job situation, so listen closely to what they say. Different perspectives are just what you need.

Tuesday 14th

There could be a surprise coming your way, and it is most likely to be a positive one. It could be that your friends throw you a surprise party or are the alibi for a surprise your partner is planning for you. Expect the unexpected today.

Wednesday 15th

Today could bring up a major change, or at least some intensity in your relationship. The energy is neither good nor bad, but it requires your ability to bring balance. Luckily, you are emotionally grounded and can seek advice from your friends if necessary.

Thursday 16th

After the last few busy days, you now seek some time for yourself. Your colleagues might be surprised that you seem a little distant, so just let them know it is not about them and you simply need some time to recharge. Try to create a space for meditation or contemplation.

Friday 17th

Try not to brood too heavily, instead focus on your inner and outer beauty. If you can go for a wellness retreat, visit a spa, have a massage or a facial you could make great use of the energy. It is an amazing day to celebrate your own beauty.

Saturday 18th

The Moon moves into Cancer, and you feel fresh and new. You allow your emotions to ebb and flow just like the tides of the sea. Be aware that it can be a little tricky for others, and show compassion if they cannot handle your moods easily.

Sunday 19th

Your mind and feelings are perfectly aligned. You feel in synch with yourself and nature. If you can spend the day by the sea or pool you will be able to recharge even more. Any kind of water will always help to soothe you and bring a relaxing vibe.

Monday 20th

Very rarely, two New Moons take place in the same sign. In 2020, it happens in Cancer. This cosmic occurrence helps you to set a conscious intention instead of a mere wish. You surely received lots of clarity during the last month, so think about where you want to be in six to twelve months from now. You have the ability to make it happen.

Tuesday 21st

Today could be very emotional, as it is the last day of the Sun in Cancer. Review the last month since the solstice and write down everything that has changed, shifted and happened in your life. Finish this exercise with a gratitude journal, listing at least ten things you are grateful for.

Wednesday 22nd

There was a lot of value in the experiences of the last month. Over the next thirty days, you will have a closer look at your self-worth and the value of your possessions. There might be things you have outgrown or simply no longer have use for. Where do you need an upgrade?

Thursday 23rd

You will be keen to declutter right now. The best approach is to consider which of your possessions are useful – or not. Objects that you never use, or those that are broken, should be the first to sort through. If you have a hard time deciding, create three piles: recycle, charity shop and keep.

Friday 24th

Today is a day where an illusion might crack. It is not an easy process to be completely honest with yourself, but as soon as you realise what keeps your fantasy from being a reality you can act accordingly. Dreams can come true if you ground them in reality.

Saturday 25th

This weekend, you would rather stay at home than go out. Maybe you want to invite your extended family over and have a party? You know you are a great host, and you love to take care of everyone. Whether it's a summer barbecue or formal dinner party, the choice is yours.

Sunday 26th

A family is not only a safe place, it is also mirror-like. Sometimes we do not like what is reflected back at us. If a little tension arises today, be reassured that it will pass by quickly. There's no need to worry, and remember not to take it personally.

Monday 27th

Another busy week is ahead and today is no exception. Career choices lie ahead, and you try your best to combine them with the vision of your future self. These decisions are important ones, but you do not have to rush into making a choice right away. Think it all over.

Tuesday 28th

Jupiter and Neptune are locked in a pleasant conversation, so there are good future and relationship vibes. This boosts the loving energy around you, and makes you aware of your priorities. You want things to flow easily, and for there to be more love in your life. How can you bring more love to others too?

Wednesday 29th

A long time ago, Venus started her journey in your subconscious and helped you to discover and redefine your inner and outer beauty. Now she finally enters new territory. Are you satisfied with your makeover? Did you imagine yourself to ever be so beautiful?

Thursday 30th

As you take care of daily routines, your mind becomes free to flow. You will finally understand what you must do in order to expand the love in your life. You take great pleasure in nurturing others and, having learnt how to nurture yourself, are now able to give even more.

Friday 31st

The energy is perfect for a Friday. The first half of the day is made for you to keep up with all your necessary tasks, while the other half is perfect for enjoying time with your loved ones. Whether you go out or stay home is up to you.

AUGUST

. . . .

Saturday 1st

You are thinking about change and transformation, and also about how to deepen your main relationship. The art is to merge with your partner without losing yourself in the process. It is a fine line to walk, but you will know how to do it.

Sunday 2nd

Beware and be aware. Today has the potential to be quite dramatic. It could be that you are creating a fuss to get noticed or it could be that someone else is demanding attention – and you might not want to give it to them. If you are the one feeling ignored, you may turn cold and detached.

Monday 3rd

Happy Full Moon in Aquarius! This Moon highlights your need for intimacy, and your new approach regarding shared resources. You have already made some changes that created a win-win situation this year, and now you can reap the first rewards. There could literally be some unexpected money that comes in.

Tuesday 4th

There is a lot of restructuring taking place this year.
While you think about the structures and commitments
it really takes to establish the highest level of security
in your relationship, know that there is a tendency for
sudden surprises. Did you integrate the thoughts about
your self-worth yet?

Wednesday 5th

Mercury has been in Cancer for months and is now
finally moving onto your second house, which deals with
values, worth and possessions. Where there is Leo, there
can be a little drama, but also a feeling of royalty. Choose
royalty and avoid the drama as much as you can.

Thursday 6th

As Venus finally meets with the north node, you receive
the last important insight into your self and discover
another level of your beauty. It will be your mission to
nourish this beauty, and to become one with it. This will
help you to shine your light in the world.

Friday 7th

Venus is now transiting your first house, so other people are likely to appreciate you greatly. You will be focused on harmony and beauty within yourself, as well in your outward appearance. If you are looking to alter your outfit or haircut to something more suitable this is a great time.

Saturday 8th

Even though it is the weekend, there will be a situation that calls for you to be out in public. You will feel highly appreciated and valued for all the efforts you have made recently. You have worked hard to achieve this, so simply enjoy the recognition.

Sunday 9th

The energy flows a little uneasily today. Some tension could arise with your partner, who had hoped to spend time with you alone instead of having to share you with others or work. However, do not be made to feel guilty. There is a time for everything.

Monday 10th

You start the week eager to connect and have a good time. You could find yourself organising a get-together or receive an unexpected invitation, which you should definitely accept. Wherever you find yourself today, you will help to create a loving and relaxing atmosphere.

Tuesday 11th

There is a nagging craving for recognition inside of you and, if you are not aware of it, it may make you invent a little drama just for the sake of attention. Instead of throwing a tantrum, try to trust your self-worth and that others value you as much as you deserve.

Wednesday 12th

For the last few days you have been busy going out and connecting, and you have loved being the centre of attention. Now you want to step back, and might even start to decline some invitations. Others could be surprised by this sudden shift, but they also know you will be back soon.

Thursday 13th

You might have to make a decision today regarding your career changes. You will likely not want to make this choice right away, and you don't have to. Be assured that you have time until late December. By then, you will know all the facts and be ready to act. Don't rush.

Friday 14th

It would be great if you could take the day off from work today. If you cannot, try to get as much time for yourself as possible. There is so much to contemplate about what actions you want to take in regards to your job. It is not yet a time to act.

Saturday 15th

You are grateful that the weekend is here, and your mood softens with it. You know what you'd most like to do, and that is go to the beach. The sea gives you a sense of home, so listen to the ocean waves and be soothed.

Sunday 16th

Hopefully you were able to recharge yesterday, as today has the potential for a little more tension. You try to reconcile your legacy with your partnership and your own needs, whilst elsewhere there could be sudden changes with friends. Only one thing is for sure today; it will not be boring.

Monday 17th

You are ready to show off this Monday and stand in the spotlight. So whatever might come up in a situation where you are usually silent, today you will speak up. Others will be surprised by your sudden self-confidence, but you might be surprised even more.

Tuesday 18th

Tonight features the New Moon in Leo, and with this, you have the ability to plant a new seed of self-value and recognition about your life. Where do you want to be seen and heard? Sudden opportunities could come to you through friends and social groups.

Wednesday 19th

Fortunately, the Moon makes it to Virgo once a month, giving you a very realistic view on your current reality. Sometimes, you are so involved in your own emotions that you cannot see clearly. Right now you see what is working and what is not, and can cut out anything that is unnecessary.

Thursday 20th

What is real and what is fake? What is just a wonderful bubble of imagination, and what could be grounded in reality? You will answer these questions soon. For today, you can dwell on your dreams or watch a movie that enhances your imagination.

Friday 21st

Get prepared for a huge reality check. Mercury moves into Virgo, so you will have a great capacity to reorganise and restructure your life. Anything imperfect will not sustain. The first critical look is at home and family. What is really going on?

Saturday 22nd

The Sun joins Mercury in your third house, so you will be able to quickly implement whatever your mind discovers. This transit will set you up perfectly for the remainder of the year. A lot has already happened and there is even more to come.

Sunday 23rd

In contrast to all the recent seriousness and change, have some fun this Sunday! If there are children in your life, they could help you to relax and play. Alternatively, turn towards your inner child and indulge in the activity you enjoyed most throughout childhood.

Monday 24th

Do your career choices and actions really support your rooting structure and foundation? This is the question that keeps you busy today. In your social group, there could be a sudden opportunity to enhance your self-expression and creativity.

Tuesday 25th

Luckily, you can take a breath and focus on simple matters today. Sometimes, it is the greatest adventure to focus on your daily routine and see what treasures it holds. Be grateful for all the little things, and especially grateful for your wonderful relationships.

Wednesday 26th

Today might not be the most exciting, but it could herald a beautiful moment with your loved one. There might be a habit or routine that you no longer want to hold on to. This could be as simple as washing the dishes immediately, but could also be something related to your health.

Thursday 27th

Love is in the air. Your partner might be mesmerised by you today. You radiate a special beauty, so don't be surprised if you find yourself being stared at. Create some space, just for the two of you, and indulge in this magical moment.

Friday 28th

It is very likely that you will either receive or give an invitation to an event today, one that you want to enjoy with your partner. This could be something like seeing a movie, going to the theatre, opera or a concert. It will be something you share together, whilst surrounded by many others. What would you like to do?

Saturday 29th

Get ready for a busy, but happy, day. You tune into the structures, growth and potential of your relationship, and examine it closely. You have nothing to fear, as you've already invested a lot of work here, and will always be willing to do so again.

Sunday 3oth

It is the ultimate dreams-versus-reality kind of day.
However, you can easily balance the two and are able
to consider something unusual that could make your
dream achievable. Venus is in opposition to Pluto and
asks you for further evolution. What will this next
change be?

Monday 31st

You will have another idea about how to combine
resources and forces for a career or legacy project. Wait
a few days before you share your thoughts, and make
sure you check all the facts. This could revolutionise the
way you work, and even help you to establish something
in the world.

SEPTEMBER

....

Tuesday 1st

Change is the theme for today. You may start a checklist on what you want to transform in your relationship, followed by a step-by-step plan for how to make the changes happen. It may sound methodical, but as long as it works and supports your vision it is good.

Wednesday 2nd

Happy Full Moon in Pisces! You have already invested lots of time in your dreams and visions this year, and can now see the results so far. You are about to manifest your vision and bring every area of your life into alignment.

Thursday 3rd

Time for a reality check. Look closely at the structure and foundation of your closest relationships. This would usually mean your life partner or family members, but today it concerns a business partnership or a colleague. How could the both of you work together more effectively?

Friday 4th

The demands of your job could prove to be overwhelming today. Try to maintain your integrity, and do not be forced into doing anything that makes you feel uncomfortable. There is a way to balance this out, but it requires another shift to happen. Feel proud for noticing your own needs.

Saturday 5th

Mercury moves out of Virgo and enters Libra, so after all the recent reality checks you can start to focus on your home and family life. This will be especially significant, as your home is your retreat and your castle. To have everything in order here is a high priority for you.

Sunday 6th

It is time to shine and show off! Venus has just moved into your second house and, with the Moon in Taurus, you are out in public, meeting with friends or engaging in a social activity. You will likely stand in the spotlight today.

Monday 7th

A friend could come round with a surprise for you or your partner. There lots of good vibes, and appreciation is especially in the air. Enjoy this attitude of gratitude. Later in the day, you may have a surprise for your friend in return.

Tuesday 8th

Pay close attention during talks with your friends. Even if you just listen, and are not actively involved in the conversation, something really important could come up that will help you cherish the relationships in your life even more. You could give great advice too.

Wednesday 9th

The Sun makes a wonderful and flowing connecting to Jupiter, bringing lots of luck. If you don't usually buy a lottery ticket, buy one today. Elsewhere, this is a great day to surprise a loved one with a gift. It doesn't need to be lavish, just thoughtful.

Thursday 10th

You recently noticed that changes are necessary in your career and legacy. Mars moves retrograde in this area for the next six weeks, so use this time to reconsider and re-evaluate what it is you truly want. Sit tight, and think over the options.

Friday 11th

When the Moon moves into Cancer, you usually feel good. However, today you are occupied with questioning your dreams. It is important not to fall for illusions, but it is not necessary to give up on dreaming. Spark your imagination by watching a true-story movie with a happy ending.

Saturday 12th

This weekend asks you to focus on your needs, as well as the way you participate in your relationship. You need to give enough to yourself so that you can act and give freely in your relationship. Otherwise, the expectations you set on your partner are too high and cannot be fulfilled.

Sunday 13th

This is an interesting Sunday. Jupiter has finished its retrograde motion and moves direct. Get ready for more growth in your relationship, which will lead to greater depth in the future. You will also be thinking about your need for self-actualisation in regards to your job. Try not to overreact to anything today.

Monday 14th

Choose something extravagant from your wardrobe. Today, you want to be seen and heard. With the Sun in a positive connection to Pluto, you could be in a powerful position in your immediate surroundings, such as your neighbourhood. You will make good use of that power, and try to get it right for everybody involved.

Tuesday 15th

Some of your friends could be jealous about your newly found self-confidence. They are not used to you standing in the spotlight, but do not be irritated by them. Instead, see it as a compliment and try to inspire them to be confident themselves.

Wednesday 16th

Today the energy might feel flat, so it is okay if you need some time to rest. Just do the work that is necessary and to an acceptable standard. If it isn't perfect, that's fine. Sometimes you can keep it simple and functional.

Thursday 17th

Thanks to the New Moon in Virgo, you can now begin to plant a fresh reality within your immediate surroundings. How could you promote communication in your neighbourhood? A better connection will strengthen the community, and make you love your home even more.

Friday 18th

Today you will take a look at the communication structures in your life. You will find a way to communicate more openly and honestly. You won't beat around the bush, and will get right to the point and speak your truth. This is sometimes uncomfortable, but it helps to resolve issues much faster.

Saturday 19th

Something is brewing. Once again you will try to reconcile your relationship, work and home life, but it seems like one part always comes up short. There is not much you can do about it today, but this challenge will play a major role in the upcoming decision about your career.

Sunday 20th

Time for some fun and creativity. With the Sun still in Virgo, you could create a game involving communication. Tap into your inner child and get your friends involved too. They might be surprised at first, but they will end up having just as much fun as you do.

Monday 21st

This week, you will be wise to complete any unpleasant tasks right away. You will see how much can be achieved, whilst being in the perfect mood to appreciate that. Your focus will shift by the end of the week, so be productive while you can be.

Tuesday 22nd

Home sweet home. The Sun moves into Libra, your area of home and family life. Nothing is more sacred to you than where you live. With the Sun in this area, you could start to beautify your home or consider moving to a new property.

Wednesday 23rd

There could be a useful discussion today regarding your home life, and the restrictions and responsibilities you have. Make sure all responsibilities are shared equally in your household. Everybody can participate, even children. It is not all down to you, even if you like to take the lead.

Thursday 24th

You want to spend some time with your beloved today, or perhaps want to go out and meet with some friends. On the other hand, you ponder about the perfect solution for a work and family conflict. You might not find the answer immediately, but persist with it. Make sure you still consider your own needs.

Friday 25th

You can relax much more today, and will likely enjoy some wonderful leisure time with your partner or family. You might want to stay at home, sit outside and watch the stars. There is much you can be grateful for, so be sure to let your partner or family know just how much you appreciate them.

Saturday 26th

Today may see you and your partner discussing different ways to invest in your home. You may be considering renovation works, and should be able to find consent easily. New furniture or accessories are another possibility. Either way, you are likely to find yourself at the shops looking for inspiration.

Sunday 27th

Following yesterday's chats about revamping your home, you are in the mood to get started on all the changes. Let your creativity run free and share all the tasks with your partner or family. Once your work is done, or as a little break, treat yourself to a delicious meal as a reward.

Monday 28th

You may want to drift away and escape reality today. If your recent home renovation project is not yet finished, add a hint of fantasy to one room. Imagine something that involves a mermaid, a water tank or at least some seashells.

Tuesday 29th

Finally, this is the moment you have been waiting for. Saturn, the most responsible planet in the zodiac, is done with its retrograde and ready to move forwards. Your relationship structures will improve for the final time, and then the real change will take place.

Wednesday 30th

The energy is high today, as a conflict with your career and legacy arises. Play it cool and don't overreact. Try not to react at all if possible, and instead respond once you have some distance. Emotions will run too high if you do not keep a clear head, and that will not serve the situation.

OCTOBER
····················

Thursday 1st
Today's Full Moon in Aries shines a light on your career and legacy, as well as your current work-in-progress project. Mars, the ruler of Aries, is currently retrograde so a change is about to happen. Take a closer look now to establish what exactly needs to shift.

Friday 2nd
Your recent craving for admiration lessens as Venus moves into Virgo. You'll now want to enhance and optimise all communications, and make sure you are able to serve your neighbourhood and community. The focus is more on others than on you, which will feel deeply satisfying.

Saturday 3rd
This weekend might be the first opportunity you have to be of service to your community. It is possible that you'll invite neighbours round or you might start planning a street party. It is okay if you take on a leadership role, but just make sure you do not do everything on your own.

Sunday 4th

One thing should not be missed today and that is having some fun! Life is serious enough, and everybody enjoys a good laugh in excellent company. Be the one who makes the first step and get your friends together. Solving a mystery might also be on your to-do list.

Monday 5th

Pluto, the planet of change, transformation and power, turns direct today. This means another layer of transformation has taken place, and you can now start to integrate these changes. Your hard work will start to pay off, but it is not over yet.

Tuesday 6th

It's time to retreat and rest. Whenever you step back this month, it is possible that you may do so even from your family. This doesn't need to alarm you. Sometimes, it is important to simply take care of yourself and nobody else.

Wednesday 7th

Your emotions could feel intense today, and there could be sudden outbursts if you don't find a way to express them consciously. If you are able to release your feelings through writing, singing, dancing or exercise then you should be able to get through the day easily.

Thursday 8th

You still want to withdraw, and are most likely not in the mood to have visitors or go out. You could possibly want to share some of your thoughts with a family member or call a close friend. Your diary would make a great companion too.

Friday 9th

Today's energy is not as easy as you, because Mars is in a strained aspect with Pluto. This is about intensity, and you could feel like you want to make a change right now. However, you do not yet have all the information needed to move ahead with your career choices. Stay patient.

Saturday 10th

You are balancing yours and your partner's needs very easily now. You've invested a lot to make this happen, so should feel proud that you've made it this far. A happy surprise might be on the horizon as friends come over to visit or you receive an invitation.

Sunday 11th

Even a tense Sun-Jupiter aspect can hold something positive. Today it will let you expand your family and home life with your partner. Perhaps you haven't been living together and decide to do so now, or there are other options that allow your bond to deepen.

Monday 12th

What about your possessions? Do you want to get something new for your home, or do you have everything you need? If you do decide to get something, make sure it is of high value and useful at the same time. It could have a sense of luxury too.

Tuesday 13th

You could feel challenged today as you try to find harmony between home and career. You know your priorities, and you love your home, but there has to be a way to find just the right amount for both in your life. Maybe there is an opportunity in your immediate environment?

Wednesday 14th

Situations seem to be overly complicated sometimes, and that is especially the case when you want to find solutions to several issues at the same time. There is a deep urge for you to express more fully, and to find a way to take advantage of this Mercury retrograde.

Thursday 15th

The energy is pretty low today, but you need to push through the day. Do not get involved in power games, especially at home or with your family. The tension will soon ease, so be the bigger person and exercise forgiveness and compassion.

Friday 16th

Happy New Moon in Libra! This event concerns your home and family, as well as your ancestors and roots in general. This would be a perfect time if you want to honour your ancestors or create a family tree. Tell your loved ones how important they are to you.

Saturday 17th

Today could be tricky, but also very interesting. In your contemplation about a new level of self-expression, you leave no stone unturned and search relentlessly. Be ready for some interesting revelations and ideas from your friends.

Sunday 18th

Commitment is very important to you, especially in your family and relationships. Maybe you want to make further promises to your partner, or you need to negotiate some things in a new way. The result should be a solid foundation and structure that you can build your future upon.

Monday 19th

There is another conflict brewing in regards to the actions, responsibilities and growth in your relationship. Your partner, or even you yourself, might fear that you are too busy with work. There could be several solutions, such as working less or working together.

Tuesday 20th

You suddenly want your daily life to be more exciting, so will start investigating how your social circle and friends could make it more colourful. If you are able to connect deeply with a particular friend, you might be able to express a wider range of your innermost self.

Wednesday 21st

Venus is in a happy conversation with Pluto, so you will be able to find support in your immediate surroundings. Maybe a neighbour watches the dog or babysits the kids so that you can have some quality time to spend with your beloved. Enjoy the depth of your connection.

Thursday 22nd

The Sun moves into Scorpio and that is always a special time of the year. The energy draws back, and becomes focused more inwardly and intensely. Make sure you create time and space for fun, and try not to suppress any feelings. Create an outlet for any feelings you do have.

Friday 23rd

Today is about emotional depth versus emotional distance. It is hard for you to step back emotionally, and you can become pretty upset if somebody else seems to detach. Try not to feel hurt, and instead consider that perhaps the other person just uses this as a protective mechanism.

Saturday 24th

Communication is key for you in order to enhance
the foundation your relationships are built on. If you
analyse the way you communicate, you might find that
there is the potential for improvement – not only with
your partner or family, but also with your colleagues too.

Sunday 25th

The Sun and Mercury embrace today, and you receive
a deep and transformational insight. You thought you
already knew the best way to express yourself and your
sometimes-intense emotions, but you might come up
with a brand-new outlet. Art could play a major role here.

Monday 26th

The energy flows easily, and connects your core as well
as your heart and mind. It is a wonderful way to start
the week, and all conversations might be deep and
comforting at the same time. Use this flow of energy to
get as much done as you can.

Tuesday 27th

It might be time to get out your dream journal and
make some notes about your dreams. They could be
very powerful and insightful and hold a special message.
You should also check your vision board, and add your
newest insights and adaptions.

Wednesday 28th

Two planets move into your area of home and family.
Mercury moves in retrograde motion, as if to make
sure he hasn't forgotten to look at your roots and
foundations. Meanwhile, Venus just moves in ready to
bring more love to your home and family.

Thursday 29th

It is as though there are two hearts beating in your
chest. One that seeks public recognition and success at
work, and one that holds your home and family dearly,
and would sacrifice anything for them. Do not give up
on finding a solution. You are still collecting facts.

Friday 3oth

You need to finish something at work and give it your
undivided attention, but the pressure will seem to fall
off as soon as the working day is over. You will be eager
to let off steam, so try to arrange some kind of post-work
event with your friends.

Saturday 31st

The Full Moon in Taurus could be a bit tricky today,
with lots of surprises lurking around. Elsewhere, the
wonderful connections you have throughout your social
circles are highlighted. Throw a Halloween party for
all of your friends, and be grateful for the magic you
create together.

NOVEMBER
. . . .

Sunday 1st
If you thought only Halloween was about trick or treat, you are likely to be shown otherwise today. This is a day to expect the unexpected, so be prepared to change your plans and stay flexible. Remember, surprises can be positive too.

Monday 2nd
Although you love to connect with friends, the time inevitably comes when you want to retreat and recharge. It is not the perfect alignment when this need coincides with the start of the week. Just do your best and show up, that is enough.

Tuesday 3rd
Today you can use the time you have on your own to come closer to a solution regarding your career and family conflict. You might have a really good idea, but it is not yet time to share it. Instead, write it down and contemplate a little more.

Wednesday 4th

Mercury retrograde is over, which means you did enough rethinking, re-evaluating and reflecting on your self-expression. You are now sure what you need in your home environment and from your family, and can start to integrate your insights into your day-to-day routines.

Thursday 5th

You connect with your emotions easily today. You would love to follow the natural flow, but you still have some obligations and responsibilities that you must tend to. Make sure you have enough leisure time later on, and use it to just follow your feelings.

Friday 6th

Remember to meet your own needs first. This is easier said than done, as both work and your partner are being demanding. If you can tell your partner what you want, you will get it. All you need to do is speak up, so don't be afraid.

Saturday 7th

Self-worth and self-expression are the themes for this weekend. Tension is brewing, and it could easily provoke some drama. However, this will only be a problem if you seek validation from others. The only approval you need comes from within. Focus on self-love instead.

Sunday 8th

Let this Sunday be a day full of life and vitality. You will want to show off and be seen, so why not dress in your most daring clothes? You could maybe even start to create a play. Your inner child will thank you for bringing some fun in.

Monday 9th

You are still trying to find a way to harmonise your home and career life. Today could get you further along on this path, as you start to analyse what yin and yang sides of yourself need to be perfectly balanced out. Begin by creating a checklist.

Tuesday 10th

Mercury is at the final degree of Libra today, which means your mental focus will sit intensely on your home and family life. You now know exactly how you want it to look. Later on in the day, you will be ready to focus on your self-expression.

Wednesday 11th

This Wednesday is perfect for clear communication of any kind, and it can be especially helpful for having an open talk with your loved ones. Once everything is said and heard in the most objective manner, you can enjoy some cosy time together.

Thursday 12th

This is a beautiful and powerful day. You enjoy being with your family and having the protection of your home, while Jupiter and Pluto conjunct for their third and final time. This is the last deepening and expansion within your relationships.

Friday 13th

There is the possibility of an issue with your family and your partner today. However, you and your partner will manage to resolve it perfectly, leaving you with a stronger bond than before. Your family will also be forgiving, so no hard feelings will remain.

Saturday 14th

You have been contemplating the changes necessary in your career for a long time, and now you can finally start to move forwards with your plans and take action. Mars stops its retrograde movement and turns direct, so it will take a moment before you can see change happen.

Sunday 15th

Happy New Moon in Scorpio! Scorpio is always connected to intensity and self-reflection. Your emotions could be stronger than usual, but this is also a perfect opportunity for you to go deeper in your feelings and start with a new creative outlet. Have you considered painting or dancing?

Monday 16th

You could be tempted to escape the world by staying at home and spending time with your partner. However, there are a lot of important tasks to complete today that cannot wait. Even the most beautiful things in life ask for moderation.

Tuesday 17th

Today you could meet with friends who are able to connect some dots for you. It is possible they know the right people to help get your creative outlet started. You may soon find yourself with a new group of people who share your passion.

Wednesday 18th

Beware that your actions could lead to some difficult feelings today. If you become impatient or too forceful at work, your colleagues may hold it against you. Just take a deep breath and count to ten. Save the talking for tomorrow, when it will work out much better for you.

Thursday 19th

You will be able to get to the root of an issue today and solve it, thanks to your amazing relationship skills. You will also be able to connect everyone, and remind them of their responsibilities. Together you can work out a structure for handling this issue, should it arise again.

Friday 20th

Expect the unexpected is a motto you need to take very seriously today. The energy is quite frantic, and someone needs to remain level-headed. You can be that person if you are able to detach from your feelings a little. At least try not to add to the friction.

Saturday 21st

As the Sun moves into Sagittarius, it is the time of year where you start to change things around in regards to your health and daily routine. You will want to explore different things, so you could end up cooking new and exotic dishes to integrate into your repertoire.

Sunday 22nd

Your imagination is especially vivid today, and you could find yourself orchestrating a beautiful event for your family and loved ones. There are no limits to what you can create, as the fun and joy you feel and express take priority. Don't hold back.

Monday 23rd

Monday morning is here again. You are focusing on your vision and have amazing ideas about how to embellish it even further. While you are high on imagination, you may want to talk about it and get others interested. This way they can support you, by making your dream come true.

Tuesday 24th

It is time to take action. You might have recently found a way to combine your work in the world with your vision and creative expression. What you need to do now is carry this spark of imagination with you, as it will help you to move forwards.

Wednesday 25th

If you are ever in doubt about what you want to achieve, think about how you want to feel. Tune into these feelings and focus on your intuition. This way you will know exactly what you have to do, when to act and when to surrender.

Thursday 26th

This is likely to be a very action-packed day. It is possible that you will get a lot done, just as long as you don't get distracted by any personal conflicts that may arise. These are nothing serious, just little sensitivities. You can spend your day supporting others or getting things done. You choose.

Friday 27th

There might be an interesting twist in today's plot. It will start as a typical working day, but then a sudden opportunity could put you in an unexpected scenario by the evening. For example, you might find yourself out dancing when you had planned on a night in front of the TV.

Saturday 28th

You will want to share your creative endeavours in your social circle, whether this is something planned or spontaneous. You won't be spending the day on your own, and might meet different friends or stay with the same group throughout the day. Fantasy is always in great demand.

Sunday 29th

During the day, there could be important conversations leading to new opportunities in your life. Everything seems to align to ensure your maximum growth and expression. After such an exciting weekend, make sure you take some much-needed rest and me-time in the evening.

Monday 30th

The month ends with a Full Moon lunar eclipse in Gemini, leaving you contemplating deeply about the year so far. You can feel the spirit of something new and exciting waiting in the wings. Create some space to reflect, and write down all the important steps so far.

DECEMBER

....

Tuesday 1st

Can you believe December is here? With Mercury coming into your sixth house, you will be willing and able to focus on daily business, except with a twist. You will likely change some routines and habits during that transit. The quirkier the better.

Wednesday 2nd

This will most likely be a quiet day for you. You have no interest in going out to buy Christmas gifts, and hopefully all your festive parties are scheduled for later in the month. If you do have a function to attend, make your excuses and stay home. Soul-searching should be your priority.

Thursday 3rd

Make sure your needs are met at work today. You want to give your best, but others may take advantage of your strong work ethic. If you can, stand your ground and you just might earn some respect in return. Pat yourself on the back.

Friday 4th

You will need to take care of yourself constantly throughout today. You love to support and nurture loved ones, and there is a great demand for you to do so. You try your best to make the grade. By the evening, you deserve to spoil yourself with a generous treat.

Saturday 5th

It's time to show up and be present! If there is a job vacancy you wish to apply for, do so. You will likely make a very good impression and speak convincingly about your skills. Do not waste this opportunity, and remember to be fully aware of your self-worth.

Sunday 6th

It sounds like a strange pursuit for a Sunday, but you should spend the day checking on your finances. With the Sun in your sixth house and the Moon in your second, it is important that you have an overview of what is coming in and what is going out. Adjustments may need to be made.

Monday 7th

It is a great day for Christmas plans and preparations. Who will visit whom and when, what food needs to be ordered, which gifts need to be bought and wrapped. It sounds like a lot of hard work, but it will actually feel like fun.

Tuesday 8th

You enjoy communicating with your friends and partner, and you might even want to plan a short trip away. Ask about their preferences, but be sure to consider your own. Maybe this would make a great Christmas gift? After all, what is more valuable than time spent together?

Wednesday 9th

Is it time to put up the Christmas decorations in your home? Chances are, it is one of your favourite traditions. However, be wary of taking over. Let everyone help with hanging baubles and stringing up lights. Your family will truly appreciate the chance to get involved.

Thursday 10th

If you are currently dealing with something that sounds
too good to be true, it probably is. Be a little sceptical
and suspicious. There is more than meets the eye to this
situation, and you will get a grasp on it. Just wait and see
before you jump right in.

Friday 11th

You could receive good news regarding a job application
or interview. Your daily routines will need to change if
you accept the position, but sometimes that is exactly
what is necessary to move away from bad or outdated
habits. It is the right decision if you feel passion and
excitement towards it.

Saturday 12th

Everything seems to turn out in your favour today.
Just enjoy this Saturday knowing that you are on the
right path and moving towards your future. In order
to welcome something new, you must let go of the old.
Trust yourself and your intuition.

Sunday 13th

This will likely be a quiet Sunday, as usual. The energy is a little low and flat because there is a New Moon brewing. Enjoy some quiet moments and introspection. Maybe the magic silence of a snowy day will add to your experience.

Monday 14th

Today's New Moon in Sagittarius is potent, and marks the start of a new cycle in your life. Maybe you will realise today what the future has in store for you. Make sure you consciously let go of the old and set an intention for the new.

Tuesday 15th

Who would have thought that December would be such a wonderful time for a new beginning? You are raring to start. Venus now enters your area of routine and everyday life, so she will make this even more beautiful. Quality time with your partner will also be possible today.

Wednesday 16th

As you and your partner start to dream about your future together, you will connect on an even deeper level. Your relationship has brought much healing into your life, and you now know how you want to take it further. Just enjoy the love.

Thursday 17th

Saturn leaves his home sign of Capricorn and enters Aquarius again today. Cast you mind back to what happened to you in late March, the first time Saturn assumed this position. What has changed since then? This is a time for creating new structures and foundations.

Friday 18th

Another interesting and important day, as Mercury and the Sun embrace again. This event always comes with new insights and information to be revealed. In this time of new beginnings, it seems to be even more promising. The message will reveal itself over time.

Saturday 19th

Leading up to Christmas, there is as much going on in the sky as there is down here on Earth. Jupiter is on the final day in Capricorn. He has expanded all of your relationships as far as possible, and is now ready to take it all to the next level. Are you ready too?

Sunday 20th

Jupiter in Aquarius is willing to expand all your shared resources, so you could receive an influx of money during the latter half of this transit. Jupiter and Saturn conjunct, marking the beginning of a twelve-year cycle that will likely anchor in a new way of life.

Monday 21st

The Sun moves in Capricorn, marking the winter solstice. Your focus shifts to your relationships and connections of all kinds. You will most likely spend this long night on your own. If you can, wake with the Sun. It could prove to be a magical moment.

Tuesday 22nd

Despite the impending festivities, you start to focus on work. This is highly necessary, as many matters still need to be organised or prepared. Make sure you do not push your self too far or this could end up in unpleasant discussions.

Wednesday 23rd

There might be a lot of tension today, so be sure to take plenty of breaks. Also, be especially aware of your tendency towards impulsiveness. You could easily become stressed, and it would be better if nobody gets in your way. Channel your energy into action, and be careful with tools of all kinds.

Thursday 24th

The first half of the day could still be very stressful, but thankfully the universe has good timing as the Moon comes into Taurus after midday. Everybody is able to calm down, and you feel in the perfect mood for company. Sleep tight tonight.

Friday 25th

Merry Christmas! The Moon conjunct Uranus is usually known to reveal surprises, but today that may just mean your Christmas presents. There is still the possibility that a special guest may arrive. Enjoy the time with your loved ones and your partner, and have a wonderful feast.

Saturday 26th

Today might be fairly inactive, but you still want to visit your friends and family. Instead of hot discussion, the only thing you might have to face is some stubbornness. Other than that, everyone is peaceful. It is perfect for a calm day and to watch a movie marathon.

Sunday 27th

Gladly it is Sunday, and you gratefully take the opportunity for a day off. Life has been full of people, conversation and food during the last few days. Stay at home and take some time for yourself. You need some rest and a green smoothie before you get busy again.

Monday 28th

After the peace and quiet of yesterday, life picks up the pace once more. You may be in receipt of a surprise that leaves you stunned and grateful. It will make you feel humble and as though everything is exactly the way it is meant to be.

Tuesday 29th

Happy Full Moon in Cancer. This is like an early New Year's Eve, and a spectacular end to the year for you. Celebrate yourself today. Celebrate all the work you've have done, the challenges you have faced, as well as how much you have grown and evolved. Raise a glass to all that is ahead.

Wednesday 30th

As you connect with yourself and to your vision, you intuitively realise there are old beliefs holding you back. List each one and create an action plan for how you can leave them all behind. Only then can you move fully towards your future.

Thursday 31st

That was 2020, a year that started with a bang and went on to change your life tremendously. You will grow further with your new vision, whilst also being able to work and express yourself freely. Have a happy new year, and go boldly into 2021.

Cancer

. . . .

PEOPLE WHO
SHARE YOUR SIGN

PEOPLE WHO
SHARE YOUR SIGN

. . . .

The nurturing influence of Cancer makes this sign the
go-to guardian of the zodiac calendar. Teamed with their
pioneering instinct, Cancerians have been, and still are,
some of the most powerfully empathetic figures in the
world, from Nelson Mandela to Malala Yousafzai. The
emotional impression that Crabs make is notable, the
words of Nobel Prize-winning writers Pablo Neruda and
Ernest Hemingway being just two examples. Discover
the Cancerians who share your exact birthday and see if
you can spot the similarities.

June 22nd

Donald Faison (1974), Carson Daly (1973), Dan Brown
(1964), Erin Brockovich (1960), Cyndi Lauper (1953),
Meryl Streep (1949), Elizabeth Warren (1949), Kris
Kristofferson (1936)

June 23rd

Melissa Rauch (1980), Jason Mraz (1977), Zinedine Zidane
(1972), Selma Blair (1972), Frances McDormand (1957),
Randy Jackson (1956), Clarence Thomas (1948), Alan
Turing (1912), Anna Akhmatova (1889)

June 24th

Candice Patton (1988), Lionel Messi (1987), Solange
Knowles (1986), Vanessa Ray (1981), Mindy Kaling (1979),
Robert Reich (1946), Robert Downey Sr. (1936), Chuck
Taylor (1901)

June 25th

Lele Pons (1996), Sheridan Smith (1981), Busy Philipps
(1979), Linda Cardellini (1975), George Michael (1963),
Ricky Gervais (1961), Anthony Bourdain (1956), Carly
Simon (1945), George Orwell (1903), Antoni Gaudí (1852)

June 26th

Ariana Grande (1993), King Bach (1988), Aubrey
Plaza (1984), Jason Schwartzman (1980), Paul Thomas
Anderson (1970), Sean Hayes (1970), Chris Isaak (1956),
Mikhail Khodorkovsky (1955)

June 27th

Lauren Jauregui (1996), Matthew Lewis (1989), Ed
Westwick (1987), Sam Claflin (1986), Khloé Kardashian
(1984), Tobey Maguire (1975), Vera Wang (1949), Helen
Keller (1880)

June 28th

Kevin De Bruyne (1991), Markiplier (1989), Tamara
Ecclestone (1984), Rob Dyrdek (1974), Elon Musk (1971),
John Cusack (1966), Kathy Bates (1948), Mel Brooks (1926)

June 29th

Kawhi Leonard (1991), Éver Banega (1988), Nicole
Scherzinger (1978), Charlamagne tha God (1978), Marcus
Wareing (1970), Melora Hardin (1967), Gary Busey (1944),
Antoine de Saint-Exupéry (1900)

June 3oth
Michael Phelps (1985), Cheryl Tweedy (1983), Katherine
Ryan (1983), Lizzy Caplan (1982), James Martin (1972),
Phil Anselmo (1968), Vincent D'Onofrio (1959), Lena
Horne (1917)

July 1st
Léa Seydoux (1985), Liv Tyler (1977), Missy Elliott (1971),
Pamela Anderson (1967), Diana, Princess of Wales (1961),
Dan Aykroyd (1952), Debbie Harry (1945), Olivia de
Havilland (1916)

July 2nd
Margot Robbie (1990), Alex Morgan (1989), Lindsay
Lohan (1986), Ashley Tisdale (1985), Peter Kay (1973),
Jerry Hall (1956), Larry David (1947),
Hermann Hesse (1877)

July 3rd
Sebastian Vettel (1987), Olivia Munn (1980), Patrick
Wilson (1973), Tom Cruise (1962), Faye Resnick (1957),
Gloria Allred (1941), Franz Kafka (1883)

July 4th

Malia Ann Obama (1998), Post Malone (1995), Mike Sorrentino (1982), Elie Saab (1964), U.S. President Calvin Coolidge (1872), Giuseppe Garibaldi (1807), Nathaniel Hawthorne (1804)

July 5th

Dejan Lovren (1989), Tess Holliday (1985), Megan Rapinoe (1985), Pauly D (1980), Amélie Mauresmo (1979), Susan Wojcicki (1968), Claudia Wells (1966), Edie Falco (1963), Paul Smith (1946)

July 6th

Eva Green (1980), Kevin Hart (1979), 50 Cent (1975), Jennifer Saunders (1958), U.S. President George W. Bush (1946), Sylvester Stallone (1946), 14th Dalai Lama (1935), Nancy Reagan (1921), Frida Kahlo (1907), Marc Chagall (1887)

July 7th

Ashton Irwin (1994), Ally Brooke (1993), Jack Whitehall (1988), MS Dhoni (1981), Kirsten Vangsness (1972), Jim Gaffigan (1966), Jeremy Kyle (1965), Shelley Duvall (1949), Ringo Starr (1940)

July 8th
Jaden Smith (1998), Son Heung-min (1992), Jake McDorman (1986), Sophia Bush (1982), Milo Ventimiglia (1977), Kevin Bacon (1958), Anjelica Huston (1951), John D. Rockefeller (1839)

July 9th
Douglas Booth (1992), Amanda Knox (1987), Jack White (1975), Courtney Love (1964), Jordan Belfort (1962), Kelly McGillis (1957), Tom Hanks (1956), Lindsey Graham (1955)

July 10th
Isabela Moner (2001), Perrie Edwards (1993), Golshifteh Farahani (1983), Jessica Simpson (1980), Adrian Grenier (1976), Sofía Vergara (1972), Urban Meyer (1964), Marcel Proust (1871)

July 11th
Alessia Cara (1996), Caroline Wozniacki (1990), Justin Chambers (1970), Lisa Rinna (1963), Richie Sambora (1959), Sela Ward (1956), Giorgio Armani (1934), Yul Brynner (1920)

July 12th

Malala Yousafzai (1997), James Rodríguez (1991), Phoebe Tonkin (1989), Michelle Rodriguez (1978), Anna Friel (1976), Sundar Pichai (1972), Cheryl Ladd (1951), Richard Simmons (1948), Pablo Neruda (1904)

July 13th

Rich the Kid (1992), Leon Bridges (1989), Tulisa (1988), Ken Jeong (1969), Cheech Marin (1946), Ernő Rubik (1944), Harrison Ford (1942), Patrick Stewart (1940), Simone Veil (1927)

July 14th

Conor McGregor (1988), Victoria, Crown Princess of Sweden (1977), David Mitchell (1974), Matthew Fox (1966), Jane Lynch (1960), Bebe Buell (1953), U.S. President Gerald Ford (1913), Gustav Klimt (1862)

July 15th

Damian Lillard (1990), Travis Fimmel (1979), Gabriel Iglesias (1976), Diane Kruger (1976), Brian Austin Green (1973), Brigitte Nielsen (1963), Forest Whitaker (1961), Linda Ronstadt (1946)

July 16th

Luke Hemmings (1996), Gareth Bale (1989), AnnaLynne McCord (1987), Jayma Mays (1979), Corey Feldman (1971), Will Ferrell (1967), Phoebe Cates (1963), Ginger Rogers (1911), Ida B. Wells (1862)

July 17th

Billie Lourd (1992), Tom Fletcher (1985), Gino D'Acampo (1976), Gavin McInnes (1970), Jason Clarke (1969), Angela Merkel, Chancellor of Germany (1954), David Hasselhoff (1952), Camilla, Duchess of Cornwall (1947), Donald Sutherland (1935)

July 18th

Priyanka Chopra (1982), Michiel Huisman (1981), Kristen Bell (1980), Stefan Janoski (1979), Kelly Reilly (1977), M.I.A. (1975), Vin Diesel (1967), Richard Branson (1950), Hunter S. Thompson (1937), John Glenn (1921), Nelson Mandela (1918)

July 19th

Shane Dawson (1988), Jared Padalecki (1982), Topher Grace (1978), Benedict Cumberbatch (1976), Nicola Sturgeon (1970), Brian May (1947), Vladimir Mayakovsky (1893), Edgar Degas (1834)

July 20th

Ben Simmons (1996), Alycia Debnam-Carey (1993),
Julianne Hough (1988), Gisele Bündchen (1980), Sandra
Oh (1971), Anton du Beke (1966), Chris Cornell (1964),
Natalie Wood (1938)

July 21st

Maggie Lindemann (1998), Juno Temple (1989), Paloma
Faith (1981), Josh Hartnett (1978), Ross Kemp (1964),
Robin Williams (1951), Cat Stevens (1948), Ernest
Hemingway (1899)

July 22nd

Prince George of Cambridge (2013), Selena Gomez
(1992), Keegan Allen (1989), John Leguizamo (1964),
David Spade (1964), Willem Dafoe (1955), Don Henley
(1947), Danny Glover (1946), Oscar de la Renta (1932), Bob
Dole (1923)